WHEN THE SPIRIT COMES

When the Spirit Comes

Colin Urquhart

HODDER AND STOUGHTON
LONDON SYDNEY AUCKLAND

"To my Father, who made me His son."

The biblical references, unless otherwise stated,
are taken from the Revised Standard Version.

Copyright © 1974 by Colin Urquhart

First published in 1974 by Hodder and Stoughton
a division of Hodder Headline PLC

This edition 1994

The right of Colin Urquhart to be identified as the author of
the Work has been asserted by him in accordance with the
Copyright, Designs and Patents Act 1988.

10 9 8 7 6 5 4 3 2 1

A CIP catalogue record for this title is available from the British
Library.

ISBN 0 340 60380 1

Printed and bound in Great Britain by
Cox & Wyman Ltd, Reading, Berkshire

Hodder and Stoughton Ltd
A Division of Hodder Headline PLC
47 Bedford Square
London WC1B 3DP

Contents

Acknowledgments

My personal thanks to the Lord who sustained me in this task; to Caroline, His precious gift to me; to Val who has successfully pulled the book to pieces and saved you all from the irrelevant parts; and to Jeanne for countless hours at the typewriter. Thanks also to Norma for her help and to all who have allowed their personal details to be included.

FOREWORD

GOD IS FULL of surprises! When I wrote this book twenty years ago I could not have foreseen how He would use it, or what would happen to me personally in the subsequent years, except that the book would never have been written but for a series of prophetic words from God.

One of these was of a bird sitting on the peak of an exceedingly high, snow-capped mountain, an altitude far in excess of where you would expect to find such a bird. The Lord made it clear to me that this book would be like that bird; it would be at that height because He had chosen to place it there. He was going to take it and raise it to a height where it seemed it did not belong. Such words gave me the necessary encouragement to finish this writing. Never having written a book before, I was plagued by doubts as to who would want to read it. Who would be interested in what was happening in a church on the outskirts of Luton?

Since its publication I have received written and verbal testimonies from around the world, indicating that God has graciously used this little book to bless thousands. People have come to know Jesus personally, they have been baptised in the Holy Spirit and healed by God in many different ways because of the way He has spoken to them through these pages.

I have heard of whole churches being blessed because the Holy Spirit began a move of God when members read this book. People experienced first-hand what happens "When the Spirit Comes". One letter came from a remote place (of which I had never heard!) in Africa. Apparently the members of a congregation had only one copy between them. Everyone read it, or had it read to them, and God visited the church in power.

Obviously I rejoice in the way God has used this book. But I take no credit (or royalties) for this. Once a book is finished I feel almost detached from it. It is the Lord's business how He chooses to use it, and all the glory belongs to Him for whatever fruit it produces for His Kingdom. By the time a book actually appears in print I am seeking to keep up with the things God is doing subsequent to it being written!

Looking back I realise that what was happening at St. Hugh's was a move of God more akin to revival than renewal. When I left St. Hugh's to pursue the itinerant ministry to which the Lord called me, I was immediately struck by the fact that essential elements of what had happened in Luton were missing from most churches that were enjoying "charismatic renewal".

This perplexed me at first, for I had assumed that everyone open to the Spirit of God would be sharing in the same blessings. To one extent they were, but I was deeply aware that in most situations there was not the same depth of repentance, quality of love, spontaneous faith or openness of heart that we enjoyed at St. Hugh's. This saddened me, but it made me profoundly thankful for what God had done in those precious years.

However, I am careful not to look back wistfully. My main focus now is to seek God for a new move of revival that will impact the whole nation. I have known times of personal and corporate revival in the intervening years. But I remain convinced that the best is still to come.

Colin Urquhart
1994

1 God's Son

"THAT'S IT! THAT'S IT! I'm a son of God!"

It was like a great flash of light. Something I had been searching for had suddenly been discovered. "I am a son of God!"

That truth transformed my life and my ministry.

I was reading a book, *The Normal Christian Life*, written by a Chinese layman with the unlikely name of Watchman Nee. This book made me realise that nearly everything I had known and experienced about the Christian life was "subnormal".

God is wanting to do so much for His people; but I had never dared to believe that He wanted to do very much for me. I had been taught to be highly suspicious of "experience" and "subjective Christianity". God was often portrayed to be great, but remote; to be believed in, to be worshipped, but definitely not to be experienced in a personal way. What mattered above everything else was objective truth; that we believed in God's existence and His love.

Now something was happening to me; something that could only be described as "experience". I felt different. I *was* different. I was bubbling over with joy. It seemed as if the whole room, the whole house, everyone and everything around me had changed. I wanted to go dancing and skipping around the house shouting, 'I'm a son of God! I'm a son of God! I AM A SON OF GOD!"

Jesus Christ died for me — that was a truth I had known

from childhood. I had not appreciated that when He died, I died with Him. My old sinful nature had been put to death on the cross. I had been crucified with Christ, and I had never realised it. I had been unable to live the new life of Jesus, because I had not reckoned that my old nature was dead and buried with Him. My life was still dominated by the fears and anxieties of the "old" life.

Now I was set free to enjoy Jesus. My old life was dead, I need not live in subjection to the sin, the fears and doubts of the past. I was a new person, free to share a new, risen life with Jesus. I was a son of God, filled with the Holy Spirit. I knew it, not only in my head; my whole being witnessed to the fact.

I was filled with praise for God, in a way I had never known before. Words could not express the love I felt for Him.

One question remained unanswered: "Why me, Lord; why have you chosen to reveal yourself in this wonderful way? I am nothing."

When training for the ministry at King's College, London, I learned that a self-imposed discipline was necessary in the spiritual life, and I would spend many hours in meditation. Often there would be periods of silent adoration when I was conscious of God's presence.

Shortly before ordination, I went through a period of restlessness in prayer, finding it difficult to concentrate. One day in chapel I said: "Lord, I believe you want me to be ordained. You know I'm scared stiff. I cannot understand why you should want me to do this; I'm not the right sort of person. I freeze in the presence of others: I'm afraid to open my mouth at meetings. But Lord I am yours, I give myself to you. If you want me to do this you will have to provide all the power."

I became even more restless, but in a different way. I could hardly keep still and longed for Evensong to end. No sooner had we said "Amen" to the blessing than I hurried out of the chapel, raced up to my room and threw myself on to the bed.

I started to breathe very heavily for a few minutes, and then suddenly was filled with a great peace. God was breathing His Holy Spirit into me. I found myself speaking strange words, a language I did not know. It never occurred to me that this was "speaking in tongues". I did not understand it.

During the early years of my ministry at Cheshunt in Hertfordshire, I occasionally spoke "in tongues", although this still did not mean very much to me.

While at Cheshunt I began to grow dissatisfied. I would often stand in the pulpit waiting to preach thinking: "Why are all these people here?" Most of them were seeking God in their lives, but I knew that very few had actually found Him.

I became very frustrated because I felt completely incapable of helping these dear people to find the Lord. I could talk about Him; I could teach people about "the faith", but I couldn't say "Come and meet the Lord you are seeking".

Yet I felt deep within me that there must be a way for God to become real to us. "If it is true that He loves us, then He wants us to know His love, to know Him," I thought. How? The answer seemed beyond my grasp.

My frustration grew more intense when I began visiting Derek. He was in his early thirties, suffering from multiple-sclerosis, and always delighted to receive visitors in his bungalow.

"Colin, how good of you to come and see me. I know how busy you are. I really do appreciate it." It was the same kind of welcome on every visit, and each time I went, I felt worse.

"Derek, I can't do anything for you. I am completely helpless." I used to leave that bungalow feeling defeated.

While at college, Father Jim Wilson came to lecture to us about the healing ministry of the church. Something he said came back to me: "Jesus healed then, and if He is alive today, He can heal now." I believed that the Lord loved Derek: "Surely, then, the Lord must want to heal him." I thought. "God cannot want someone whom He has created and whom He loves to waste away like this."

How? Again that same question. How can the healing power of Jesus be brought to people like Derek?

A group of people met once a month in our church to pray for the sick, but it all seemed formal and life-less — reeling off a list of names to the Lord and reciting the troubles of each one of them.

Something different was needed: not just praying for sick people, but healing them!

I prayed and asked God to show me who should be the members of a prayer group that would be prepared to meet every week, and learn how to fulfil His command to "heal the sick". Tentatively, I went to each of those whom I be-lieved should form this group. I was staggered at the re-sponse I found: "I have felt that something important was about to happen." "We have needed something like this for a long time." Others were hungry for reality too.

The first group met at the home of Doug and Ruby. We learned to take hold of the healing promises of God, and to hold others in His healing presence. We soon began to see our prayers being answered and other groups being formed.

I began to minister personally to people. It was one of the most significant moments of my life when I said to someone for the first time, "The Lord will heal you." And the Lord brought healing into the life of that person.

After three and a half years at Cheshunt, I moved to be priest-in-charge of St. Thomas's, Letchworth. During my three years there, several similar groups were formed and although these were an inspiration to those who took part, we did not see many demonstrations of God's power as a result.

During my ministry at Letchworth I first experienced healing in my own life. For years I had worn glasses, with quite powerful lenses. While on holiday in North Wales with members of the church youth club, some of us were caught in a heavy rain storm. It was so bad I had to take off my glasses in order to see at all. It was some time before I realised that my vision was not blurred, neither was I seeing double! Had the Lord healed my eyes?

At the time I said nothing. On the following day, while climbing Snowdon, one of us stepped on a wasps' nest and in seconds everyone, except me, was covered with wasps.

I whisked off my anorak and started beating them away, completely forgetting that my glasses were in one of the pockets. They were now in pieces, except for one lens which had somehow remained intact.

Later I had my eyes examined by a consultant who found it difficult to believe that I could ever have used that lens. He told me that I need not wear glasses but warned me that my eyes would become tired and therefore it would be advisable to have a new pair with much weaker lenses. A Christian friend said, "You won't bother to have them, will you?"

I hesitated. "Well, I suppose I may as well if they have been prescribed." My friend looked disappointed, as well he might. The glasses were ordered, I paid several pounds for them, never wore them and later lost them.

"O ye of little faith . . ." It served me right!

This incident, coupled with the fact that everyone except me was stung by the wasps, made a deep impression upon many of the youngsters. It led to long hours of discussion, and resulted in several of them seeking the Lord.

Seeking the Lord — not finding him! I came up against the same failure and frustration as before: how to bring people into a living relationship with Jesus Christ.

"Come to church."

"It's dull and boring, except when you preach one of your funny sermons," they said.

"Pray."

"Who to? How? Why?" they said.

"Help others."

"We do — get quite a kick out of it too. But you don't have to go to church and all that just to help other people," they said. And they were right!

Slowly I began to trust God more and found that things

happened as a result. I was having to preach three, sometimes four times on a Sunday and there never seemed to be
enough time to prepare so many sermons properly.

"This is ridiculous, Lord," I said one day. "I am sure you
don't want me to spend all this time preparing sermons."

That week I prepared nothing for the evening service,
except myself. I prayed that God would speak through me. I
stood up to preach, not knowing what I was going to
say — and the words just flowed. I had always been a hesi-
tant speaker, but on that occasion there seemed to be a new
conviction in what was being said.

The congregation at the evening service began to increase. I couldn't understand why. "There's something
different about the sermons!" I was told. So that was it! No
more sermon notes, I decided. Instead prayer, prayer and
still more prayer. On Saturday evenings I would go into the
church, lock the door and prostrate myself before the altar.
"Lord, speak through me."

More young people became members of St. Thomas's and
we began to get the reputation of being a "live" church.
That could not conceal from me the fact that we needed the
Lord to be real, alive and powerful in our lives — and, for
the most part, He wasn't.

2 Coffee-Pot Christians

I LOVE CRICKET and never miss the opportunity to play. The annual Diocesan Cricket Club Dinner took place in St. Albans, in December 1969. After the meal the Suffragan Bishop of Hertford said, "How would you like a challenging job?"

"I hadn't thought of leaving St. Thomas's yet," I replied.

"That's what I told the Bishop of St. Albans, but there is a parish that might be just the right place for you."

The Bishop went on to tell me about the parish of St. Hugh, Lewsey, a new suburb of the large industrial town of Luton.

"It's a tough job. The first priest had a nervous breakdown and the present vicar's physical health has just given way under the strain. There will be a lot of hard work, and it's no use expecting much response. So we would only leave you there for five years: you'll have had enough by then."

Some prospect!

I was full of doubts about leaving St. Thomas's at first, but when I went to visit Lewsey some three or four weeks after the conversation with the Bishop, I knew that this was where God wanted me to be. In April my wife, Caroline, and I moved with our children from Letchworth to Luton.

Four weeks earlier Andrea, our third child, was born with what is commonly called "clicky hips". The lining of her hip joints was imperfectly formed causing the bones to "click",

She was put in a frame (in the form of a cross!) which kept her legs apart and prevented the hip joints from moving freely. It was hoped that over a period of a few weeks the defect would be remedied.

Three weeks after the birth Caroline took the baby to see the consultant. He shook his head sadly.

"I want you to understand that this doesn't always work," he said. "I'm afraid there are no signs of improvement."

"What does that mean?" Caroline asked.

"It means that her movement will be impaired until she is eighteen months old. She will then have surgery and will be in plaster for some time. After that she will need calipers, and will have to learn to walk."

Caroline was in tears when she came back from the hospital. There was only one thing for it — prayer.

The following week, only a day or two before our move to Luton, the consultant examined Andrea again, very thoroughly.

"Well," he said with a smile, "she seems to be fine. I'll put you in touch with the consultant at Luton who can keep an eye on her. As far as I am concerned she doesn't need that frame any more."

The other consultant confirmed that Andy's hip joints seemed sound enough. He suggested that we continued to use the frame for another few weeks "just to be on the safe side". We didn't mind that; we knew the Lord had healed her.

Andrea has developed normally and shows no signs of any physical defect four years later.

Between moving to Luton and the date of my institution as Vicar of the parish of St. Hugh, I had two weeks — time to unpack, get straight and read *The Normal Christian Life* by Watchman Nee. Time to realise that God had made me His son!

With this revelation came the awareness that I had arrived at the point to which the Lord had been gently leading me over the previous seven years. I had known the working of the Holy Spirit in many aspects of my life and ministry, especially in healing and preaching. I had experienced a relationship with God in prayer for several years, but I had never known anything like this. My heart was full of love and praise for Him.

Jesus was real in a more intimate way than ever before. Prayer was a sheer delight, for I was in communion with God in a deeper way. The Word of God, which had become more precious to me over the years, leapt to life; the Lord was speaking to me from every page.

I was feeling happy and free and full of love for those who were around me. A new kind of love. Even my love for Caroline was stronger and deeper. It is so difficult to put into words how liberated I felt. I was free to love God's people and I was free to love Him as never before.

Yet I realised that nothing extraordinary had happened to me; I had come into the experience of Jesus and the power of the Holy Spirit that God wanted for all His children. This was something to be shared with everyone. I could hardly wait to start in my new church.

St. Hugh, Lewsey, was a new parish. The church building was then only three years old, and when it was consecrated, every penny of its cost had been paid; there was no debt. A congregation of faithful communicants had worked hard together to establish the church in this new area. But there was discontent among many of the leading people.

"Is this what it is all about; raising money for new buildings, then having stewardship campaigns to support them?" I was asked.

"No," was my answer, "it's not all."

"Then what else is there?"

"Just wait and see."

None of us had to wait very long. I was longing to say to everyone: "There is more, there is more. You are a son of God. You are dead to the old life. You have a great new life within you, and the power of the Holy Spirit is just waiting to come upon you." But I had to be patient. If I was to stand up on my first Sunday and say anything like that, they would all think that they had a "nut" for a vicar.

I felt that we were all about to set out on a great adventure together. None of us knew where we were going or what the journey would be like. Deep within was the conviction that it was going to be different from anything I had known. God Himself was very definitely going to be in charge. I soon discovered that experiencing the power of the Holy Spirit in my life meant that I was also aware of God leading me in a much more positive and direct way than I had known before.

My first sermon was about Jesus walking on the water. When Peter called to Jesus from the boat: "Lord, if it is you, bid me come to you on the water", Jesus simply replied: "Come". The decision was Peter's. He could stay in the safety and security of the boat, or he could get out, keep his eyes fixed on Jesus and walk. "I am going to get out of the boat," I said, "and I hope that some of you will come with me."

We were soon to discover that it is exhilarating walking on the water with Jesus.

One week after my institution, there was a meeting of the Parochial Church Council. I asked that there be no agenda. "How can we have a meeting without an agenda?" I overheard someone say.

I spent a good part of the day in prayer. When I arrived, all the members of the council were sitting, waiting. There was an air of anticipation.

"Let's begin with prayer," I said. Everyone shuffled. "I want to share with you a different way of praying."

They looked at one another.

"I want you to relax every part of your body. Feel completely at ease." One member of the council told me some time later that he sighed inwardly at this point and said to himself, "Oh well, we had better humour him, at least for the first meeting."

Jesus said to His disciples, "My peace I give to you." I continued, "Hear Jesus saying those words to you now: 'My peace I give to *you*.' Repeat the words over and over again and feel the Lord filling you with His peace."

The Lord's peace descended upon the gathering. I fed into the silence one or two other sentences from the Word of God, and we rested in His peace together for about ten minutes. Everybody was then expecting me to give a long talk outlining my expectations for the parish. Instead I asked, "What is a Christian?"

The silence continued, but it was not such a peaceful silence as it had been. I could see from the faces in front of me what several were thinking: "What a stupid question!" "What an arrogant question!" "We know what a Christian is!"

"Would someone like to suggest an answer?" I asked.

There was still silence. Instead of looking at me, people began to look down at their shoes. They were thinking — hard! I asked everyone for a reply. Most were fairly predictable:

"A Christian is someone who believes in God."

"A Christian is someone who goes to church."

"A Christian is a good person."

"A Christian is someone who has faith."

"A Christian is someone who helps other people."

When everybody had spoken, I was obviously expected to give my answer. I only pointed out that we all seemed to have our own opinions.

"As far as I can see, they are not worth very much. Only God's opinion matters. What is His idea of a Christian? We had better find that out. All our answers tonight have been about what we do for God. I believe that a Christian is someone who allows God to do something for him."

The Lord sowed a seed in the hearts of several people that night. We had begun to face the truth.

The next few weeks were spent in visiting and getting to know the people of St. Hugh's. I asked the two curates, Michael and John, to choose fifteen members of the congregation whom they thought were spiritually hungry. I went to see each of them and invited them to a special course of meetings at the vicarage. This group, mainly men, included many members of the Church Council.

Again I spent time in prayer, for I knew that I had to lead these people into a living relationship with Jesus Christ and into an experience of the Holy Spirit. I was going to need the Lord to show me the way to do this.

The air of anticipation had been growing, especially among those who had been at that first council meeting. We began with the same question: "What is a Christian?" This time I found myself doing the speaking. For two hours I talked about Jesus and was amazed at the way the Good News poured out of me. What is more, everyone was listening.

That is not to say they all enjoyed what they heard. Cliff, one of the fifteen, later told me: "If I'd had the courage, I would have walked out halfway through, and I think most of the others would have followed. Nobody else moved, so I didn't either."

What made Cliff want to walk out? We were looking at many of our preconceived ideas of what it meant to be a Christian. It did not mean being a good person, doing things for God or trying to follow His teaching. First and foremost it meant allowing God to do something for us.

I was desperately trying to find a simple way to explain how God wants to deal with the "old life" and come pouring into our lives in the power of His Holy Spirit, when the Lord came to my rescue. He gave me an illustration that has since led to the lives of hundreds of people being transformed by His power.

Suddenly in mid-sentence, I rushed out of the lounge and into the kitchen. "A teapot. Quick! I must have a teapot!" I said to Caroline, who had just finished putting the children to bed.

'It's full of tea leaves,' she said.

"Haven't we another one?"

"What do you want it for?"

"I can't explain now. What about this old coffee-pot? I can use that."

I rushed back to the lounge with it. "Every human being

is like a coffee-pot," I began. "Imagine that there's a certain amount of liquid in this pot, representing the natural human power and resources that each of us has; our ability to work, to think, to love, to talk, to bring up our children and so on.

"Because we have free-will, we can tilt our coffee-pot in any direction whenever we please, and out of the spout will flow some of the liquid. In other words we will use some of the resources within us to do whatever we have to do. That is a human being; but not a Christian. The trouble with this character is that he can use the resources already within him, but his lid is firmly on. Nothing more can be poured into him.

"If you have ever tried to fill a pot with the lid on, you will know that the water flows over the outside of the pot, and all you get is a mess."

I went on: "Most people's spiritual lives are like that — a mess. And that can even be said of many church-goers. They try to serve God in their own strength, instead of allowing Him to remove the lid and pour His life and strength into them. This is what God wants to do for each one of us: to pour His love into us, not over us. He wants to give to us all the blessings that only He can give.

"It is obviously important that this lid is removed, because it is acting like a barrier keeping God out of our lives. No wonder the Christian life seems like a hard struggle to us, if we are trying to know Him and serve Him with our lids on!"

Everybody was following this illustration intently. I continued: "St. Paul calls this lid the 'self' — that naturally sinful, selfish, self-centred part of us that says: 'My life is my own to do what I like with. I know what I want and I am going to have what I want. I am going to be lord and master of my own life.' I ... me ... my ... self ...

"God wants to remove that lid, that old self, so that He can come flowing into our lives.

"How can this happen, so that Jesus will come pouring into us?" I sensed that this was the appropriate point at which to stop. "Come again next week and we'll discover the answer to that question."

The following Wednesday all the members of the group re-assembled, except one. Cliff told me that when he left at the end of the first session he was determined not to come again. However, all week he could not stop thinking about what had been said and when it came to the evening of the meeting, he knew he had to come.

We continued with the coffee-pot. "When we look closely at the lid, we see that it is made up of a number of different layers. There is the layer of sin and guilt — anything in our lives that is opposed to God's will. Such things act as a barrier between Him and us. There is the layer of fear, which prevents us from feeling free and from trusting God; and there is the layer of doubt.

"People often say, 'I will solve my own doubts, in my own time, in my own way.' That is impossible. Doubt is a spiritual sickness that can only be healed by God revealing Himself to us.

"All of us have guilt, fears and doubts. It is wonderful that God can remove these things that belong to the old 'self' and make the way clear for Him to come pouring into our lives in the power of His Holy Spirit."

There was a general sense of astonishment that anyone should claim that God wanted to do such things for us and would actually do them. I believed that the Lord wanted to bless others as He had blessed me, for I was nothing special!

"How can we be rid of that lid, that old nature of ours, that is separating us from God?" I continued. "By realising that we are dead!"

Some seemed perplexed, others angry.

"St. Paul says, 'Have you forgotten that when we were baptised into union with Christ Jesus we were baptised into his death? By baptism we were buried with Him, and lay dead, in order that as Christ was raised from the dead in the splendour of the Father, so also we might set our feet upon the new path of life.' (Romans 6: 3–4 NEB) We need to enter into the truth of what God has done for us in baptism. St. Paul said: 'I have been crucified with Christ; it is no longer I who live, but Christ who lives in me.' (Gal. 2:20) Each of us needs to be able to say the same."

How? It seemed the answer to that was crucifixion.

3   A Broken Lid

THE MEMBERS OF the group began to warm to the possibility that they could be drawn into a new relationship with God, through the cross. They would then know that they had "already passed from death to life". And the way would be clear for God to pour the gift of His Holy Spirit into them.

What about this Holy Spirit? We all believed in Jesus, as the Son of God who died and was raised for us. However, most of us were very uncertain what we believed about the Holy Spirit.

The disciples of Jesus came to recognise Him as the Son of God. In a very real way they experienced the cross, and they were eye-witnesses of the resurrection. Yet, when Jesus appeared to the disciples in His risen body, He commanded them not to go out and witness to Him. Instead He told them to wait until the Holy Spirit came upon them. He promised, "Before many days, you shall be baptised with the Holy Spirit" (Acts 1:5). And He added what this would mean, "You shall receive power when the Holy Spirit has come upon you; and you shall be my witnesses in Jerusalem and in all Judaea and Samaria, and to the end of the earth" (Acts 1:8).

We were terrified at the idea of witnessing and hardly ever spoke to anyone about Jesus Christ; we were too embarrassed. We had already recognised the need for God's power in our lives; now we could see that the Holy Spirit was God's power in Jesus and His disciples. We were coming to understand that God wanted to share the same empowering of the Holy Spirit with us.

Jesus wanted to remove the "lid" and pour His Holy Spirit into us; then we would be filled with Him! Great! If we continued to be filled with His Spirit, we would begin to overflow with Him. Greater still!

I was experiencing something new in my ministry: the effect that revelation has on people. Nearly everybody in that group was now not simply listening, they were sitting on the edge of their seats, eagerly longing to hear more. The questions came fast. "How can this happen?" several asked. "How can we be filled with the Spirit like that?" I avoided giving an answer — we were not ready yet! Instead I asked a question: "What do you want to be like as a person?" The Bible has a very simple answer. St. Paul says: "The fruit of the Spirit is love, joy, peace, patience, kindness, goodness, faithfulness, gentleness, self-control" (Gal. 5:22). Those are the things that God wants to see in our lives; that others want to see in us, and that we want for ourselves. They are fruit of the Holy Spirit.

The members of the group saw that there was no need for us to strive to be more loving with our human love. The Holy Spirit would cause God's love to grow in us. There was no need to create our own happiness in life; He would give us His joy. We had failed to find that peace for ourselves; we needed to receive the peace of Jesus. We all had problems of bad-temper, and here was the Lord offering to give us patience — and kindness — and goodness — and gentleness — and self-control.

"We must have more of the Holy Spirit in our lives! How?" That question again.

"Let's meet for one more week," I suggested.

Again the sense of anticipation, the longing for fresh revelation.

On the last evening, we talked about the Church as the Vine and as the Body of Christ. Jesus said, "I am the Vine, you are the branches. He who abides in me, and I in him, he it is that bears much fruit, for apart from Me you can do nothing" (John 15:5).

It was obvious that we had been doing many things in our lives "apart from" Jesus. And they were all worth nothing. He had to flow through our lives in the power of the Spirit to produce the fruit in us which would last for ever. He didn't want to bless us as separate individuals. He wanted to draw us together so that His Life could flow from one branch of the vine to another. He wanted to make us parts of His Body — the earthly, Spirit-filled Body that He needed to continue His ministry in the world. For reasons best known to Himself, He wanted us to be part of that ministry.

"You are on the spiritual level if only God's Spirit dwells within you, and if a man does not possess the Spirit of Christ, he is no Christian" (Rom. 8:9 NEB). That was the answer to our question. A Christian must be someone possessing the Spirit of Christ!

Did we possess the Spirit? We were baptised and confirmed. We had been given the Holy Spirit, and yet . . . We had already admitted that we needed to enter into the meaning of our baptism, by knowing that we were "dead in Christ". We also had to enter into the meaning of our confirmation more fully by experiencing a personal Pentecost — the Holy Spirit coming upon us in great power. The time for talking must end! God wanted to do things in our lives; we must let Him do them.

The events of the next few weeks were to have a profound effect on future events at St. Hugh's. At the end of that last session together we could have prayed and asked Jesus to fill us with His Spirit; or we could have arranged to meet together for prayer on some future occasion. Instead, I saw each member of the group individually.

The annual holiday for the local factories was about to begin, and so the personal interviews could not take place for three weeks, giving time to digest what had been said during our group meetings. We were not rushing into anything — our lives were at stake!

There was one exception. Gomer a tall, bearded Welshman, telephoned before the holiday began.

"I must come and see you," he said, "urgently."

"I have a few minutes this evening," I answered.

"Right, I'll be there."

It was early evening when Gomer barged into my study.

"It's no use," he began, "I can't wait — I must be filled with the Holy Spirit. How can I get rid of my lid — tonight!"

Gomer could be a very determined man!

Well, this is it; the crunch for me! "You talked about it Colin," I thought, "now you have to do it: lead this man to a relationship with Jesus, and to a full experience of the Holy Spirit. Lord, please help me."

"Gomer, all that belongs to that lid has to be given to Jesus."

"Right," said Gomer. "How?"

"I have to go out for about half an hour, Gomer. Go into church, sit quietly and ask the Lord to show you everything that you need to offer Him. Write it all down, the sins, fears and doubts of the past and the sort of person you are now. Open every area of your life to God, the good as well as the bad. He will take the rubbish and deal with it; He also needs to have your time and abilities at His disposal. When I come back from my appointment I will come and pray with you about all this."

"Do you mean to say you want me to write down all that lot! And then let you pray with me about it. Never!" Gomer could also be stubborn.

"If you want Jesus to fill you with His Spirit, Gomer, He needs to have all of you."

He hesitated. "Well, it had better be worth it."

"It will be," I promised.

My appointment involved me more deeply than I had anticipated, and it was about ten fifteen before I returned to the church. I hardly expected to find Gomer still there. He was — kneeling at the altar rail.

"Colin, I am such a sinner," he said as I approached,

In the following minutes, Gomer poured his heart out to God, amid his tears. I prayed that the Lord would forgive him, take away his fears, and heal him in body, mind and spirit. I laid hands on his head and prayed that the Lord Jesus would fill him to overflowing with His Holy Spirit.

There was a great sense of peace as we quietly thanked the Lord together.

"I will leave you to be alone with the Lord," I said.

Gomer didn't stay long. He couldn't keep still! He rushed home to Audrey, his wife, and Adrian, their younger son, bubbling over with joy. He told them what had happened and how wonderful Jesus was.

Gomer had become a witness. The renewal of our church had begun.

4 In The Spirit

"IT WORKS. HE'S real. I know Him. It's wonderful. It's marvellous." Gomer was losing no time in telling the others. All except one decided to open their lives to the Lord and ask for the fullness of the Holy Spirit; the holiday break had done nothing to dampen their enthusiasm.

Each person quietly prepared by "writing himself down". When we prayed together, Jesus transformed a life; another knew himself to be a son of God, filled with the Holy Spirit.

"You must have another group as soon as possible," I was told, "for our wives and husbands."

So the second "Know Jesus" group began. This time we met for four weeks; the pattern was largely the same as the first group and the interest just as great. There was no difficulty in finding another fifteen people with thirteen powerful witnesses from the first group. This second group included the two curates and our lay reader, Nick. They could hardly be left behind!

An explosion was about to take place in our church. Before my arrival, I had been told that one of the most pressing needs was to have a renewal of Christian Stewardship. A stewardship campaign had been held about two years before, but the only visible result of this had been an increase in the amount of money given.

God is concerned with every aspect of our lives, not just our money. People would freely give to the Lord, once He was a reality in their lives. So in our Stewardship Renewal, I was determined that the last thing we would talk about was money. What everybody needed was Jesus!

We recruited our lay visitors for this Stewardship Renewal from those who had been members of the first two "Know Jesus" groups. We didn't want Stewardship Renewal any more, but Spiritual Renewal!

The twenty or so people who were asked to be visitors were ready-made witnesses. And witness they did!

"We don't want to talk to you about money," they said to those they visited, "we want to talk to you about Jesus."

They testified to what had happened in their own lives and the response was amazing. On the pledge cards that were returned over a hundred people, nearly the entire congregation at that time, said that they wanted to "Know Jesus". A third "Know Jesus" group would be needed, and a fourth, and a fifth, and a sixth and a ... All in good time.

The Holy Spirit said quite clearly to me: "There's no need to rush!" He was not only encouraging us; He was also restraining us.

Another very important response came out of that renewal. Alongside the "Know Jesus" groups, other groups were starting. When I came to St. Hugh's, I missed the fellowship of the prayer and healing groups in Letchworth. It was important to begin similar groups at St. Hugh's as soon as possible. The first group met at the home of Gomer and Audrey and the first meeting there could have been a disaster!

Just before I came to St. Hugh's, Gomer had been "sacked", as he termed it, as churchwarden. He never lost an opportunity to speak his mind, and had upset some members of the congregation by his criticism of them. As a result, he was not re-elected at the annual meeting and Peter was elected in his place. Gomer was hardly speaking to Peter.

Such a broken relationship needed healing — and the only way was for them to pray together. Gomer didn't know whom I had invited to the group and he was visibly shaken when Peter walked into the house. He was still feeling deeply hurt about recent events. Nothing was said, but the atmosphere was hardly conducive to prayer! We talked about how the Word could be used to bring healing into our lives and those of others. Thankfully, as the evening progressed, the tension eased.

As the weeks passed, the tension between Gomer and Peter disappeared. In fact, three years later they were both churchwardens together!

Within a few weeks, other prayer and healing groups began. People were eager to learn how to pray. These groups were proving to be of such value that during the Renewal nearly a hundred people pledged to become members of such groups. However, the great interest in healing was also due to something else. As soon as people began to be filled with the Spirit, they began to be healed.

Stella, a school teacher and a leading member of the Church Council, was in the first "Know Jesus" group. Since the birth of her second daughter, Gillian, fourteen years previously, she had suffered from a very uncomfortable and medically incurable kidney complaint. "You will have to learn to live with the pain," she had been told by her doctor.

When the power of the Holy Spirit was released in Stella's life, she was given the faith to believe that God would heal her. We agreed to meet for prayer one day after school. When I met her in the church I said to her; "Well, Stella, its going to happen isn't it?"

"Yes," she replied with great confidence. "It is, I know it is. The Lord is going to heal me."

We prayed together, praising God for all His love and goodness. I laid hands on Stella and prayed that He would heal her. She looked radiant and just began thanking the Lord. Apart from the kidney disease, Stella was suffering from arthritis in the neck and rheumatic pains in different parts of her body. As she praised, the discomfort began to disappear.

"Oh thank you, thank you, Jesus." She was weeping tears of joy. "Thank you, thank you."

"What about the kidneys?" I asked.

"Only time will prove that they are healed," Stella said, "but I know they are. I just know it."

We continued to praise the Lord together. As we left the church, Stella could hardly walk straight. She looked drunk with the Holy Spirit. No wonder the people in Jerusalem accused the disciples of being drunk on the day of Pentecost, if they looked anything like this!

I offered to drive Stella home, but she refused.

"No, no, I want to walk without all the discomfort," she insisted.

She made it home, without being arrested! Stella was healed not only of her aches and pains, but of the kidney disease as well. Time has proved that.

Stella's healing, and others that followed, were a cause of great rejoicing and encouragement to all who were beginning to pray. The ministry of healing continued to develop in a quiet and unassuming way. Members of the congregation would come to me and ask for prayer. It was surprising to discover how many church members had physical things wrong with them! Often people told me that they would be embarrassed if others knew of the details of their ailments. I simply prayed with each individual, asking the Lord to heal His children whom He loved.

Unless there was great urgency, we always had a few days preparation before we prayed for healing. During this time we would take hold of the healing promises from the Bible, and ask the Lord to show us anything about ourselves that He wanted to change and to heal. We are told in the Gospel that Jesus healed all who came to Him. So we recognised the need for us to come to Him, to bring our whole selves to be healed, not just our physical ailments.

The adult preparation course for confirmation started as a separate "Know Jesus" group, and presented us with a problem!

Up until this time in my ministry such preparation had followed an orthodox pattern. It consisted mainly of teaching, based on the Creed, and contained, therefore, a considerable emphasis on doctrine. Now I was talking about Jesus; having a living relationship with Him and allowing Him to do what He wanted in our lives. It was Jesus, Jesus, Jesus. The result was that people wanted Jesus. Not that doctrine was discarded; in fact much more was taught and understood than ever before.

I was discovering how to lead others to Jesus and the fullness of life in the Spirit. Where did confirmation fit in? In offering our whole selves to the Lord and allowing the power of His Holy Spirit to be released in our lives, we were entering into the truth of our baptism and confirmation. We were appropriating for ourselves what God had done and what He wanted to give us through these great sacramental acts.

It seemed logical to teach the people in this group that when they were confirmed they would not only receive the gift of the Holy Spirit, but could expect the power of the Spirit to be released in their lives — as was now happening to several people in our church.

This was all very well; the length of a "Know Jesus" group was four weeks, the confirmation group lasted for ten! What frustration! After four weeks every member of the group was longing to know Jesus and to be filled with His Spirit.

"Wait," I said. "Be patient."

"What a change!" I reflected at the time. "Last year I was trying to help the group of teenagers from St. Thomas's youth club to find the Lord (and failing miserably!) and this year, after four weeks, I am straining to prevent people from discovering Him too quickly!"

That was the last time I tried to hold people back. In future years, the period of preparation was shortened and I prayed with people as soon as they were willing to offer themselves to the Lord to be filled by Jesus with His Spirit.

Life was getting pretty hectic for me personally: "Know Jesus" groups, confirmation groups, prayer and healing groups. One way or another, all these were geared to bringing people into a new life in the Spirit. Having entered that new life, how were we to grow in the life of the Spirit?

The prayer and healing groups were part of the answer. A sense of harmony and fellowship was rapidly growing in them and we were learning how to abide in the Lord in prayer. But there were two other needs that had to be met.

Being filled with the Spirit was creating a great thirst for the Word of God. We needed to study the Bible together; we also needed to learn how to "pray in the Spirit" together.

At the "Know Jesus" groups very little was said about the gifts of the Holy Spirit which Paul mentions in 1 Corinthians 12. We had been brought face to face with the fact that we needed a personal experience of Pentecost and we had noted that, in the New Testament Church, this led to the exercising of certain gifts of the Holy Spirit. The only one that had been in much evidence, as far as we were concerned, was healing.

I had told people that I spoke in tongues when praising the Lord on my own. As far as I knew, only one person in the first "Know Jesus" group had spoken in tongues as soon as he was filled with the Spirit. However, the Lord had given us all hearts of praise and as we experienced a growing need to express that praise (to tell the Lord how wonderful He was) so more of us were finding that it was impossible to do this adequately in English. We were trying to express the inexpressible.

"Lord, I want to tell you how much I love you. Help me please. Give me a language to praise you."

Because the Lord delights in the praises of His people, He readily answered the desire of our hearts.

"I've spoken in tongues!" people would whisper to me on Sunday mornings, with joy in their eyes.

"Well, praise the Lord. It's a wonderful gift isn't it?" I would reply.

"Yes, oh yes! I didn't think it was very important at first;

so many other wonderful things have happened to me. Now I
can praise the Lord more freely."

The first Bible study group was an adventure! The Word
of God was coming to life for every member of that group,
all of whom had been filled with the Spirit. God was revealing His truth to us.

At the end of the first meeting, I took the plunge. "We
need to learn to pray together in the Spirit," I began. "St.
Paul says that we should 'pray in the Spirit, and pray with the
understanding also'. We pray with the understanding, but
we don't use the prayer gifts that are available to us."

Everybody looked at me. I could tell what they were
thinking: "All right you begin!" I had never dared to speak
in tongues in public. Occasionally I had felt that it would
have been right to do so, when praying with people individually; but courage had always failed me. I thought that
instead of helping them to be healed, I would scare them out
of their wits!

When we prayed together in the Bible study group, the
reality of our Lord's presence was so great, it was as if one
could reach out and touch Him. Slowly the gifts began to be
manifested. We became free to speak in tongues, as the
Spirit led us, and began to experience the Lord speaking to
us through interpretation and prophecy.

We had thought of prophecy as being reserved for the
spiritual giants of the Old Testament, not something to be
experienced by a group of ordinary people. We now came to
understand that it is simply God speaking to His people, and
that He wanted to speak to us through this gift. The Lord
filled our mouths with His words, encouraging us and talking directly to our needs. There was only one difficulty
about those times of prayer together, and that was stopping!
Often we stayed late into the night.

Discovering what God was saying to us in the Bible was an
adventure in itself; to experience God's presence so inti-
mately and to hear Him speaking to us, was even greater.
This led to a temptation to treat the Bible study as a pre-
liminary to the real business of the evening, for we longed to

spend more time in prayer together. It was a temptation we resisted.

Some members of the group began to have what can only be described as a "ministry of prayer", and would spend a considerable time every day waiting upon God and holding people before Him.

These were great days for me: bringing people to Jesus, seeing lives being transformed by the Holy Spirit, seeing people healed, experiencing new life in the Scriptures; hearing the Lord speak when we prayed in the Spirit. They were exhausting days, but they were great!

Only one thing marred everything. My wife, Caroline, didn't want to know!

5 New Lives

NORMA TOLD ME how for eight years she had been suffering with rheumatoid arthritis, which had affected nearly every joint in her body, causing pain and stiffness. She also had two slipped discs and a virus infection in her spinal fluid. It was later discovered that the virus infection was affecting her central nervous system, and that she had a growth on her spine.

I asked Norma what hope she had been given.

"I have been told that within six months I shall be in a wheelchair for the rest of my life," she replied. Norma was forty and had a husband and two children at school.

"To be quite honest," she continued, "I have already decided that I shall commit suicide, rather than be a burden to my family."

She had not been to a "Know Jesus" group, so I talked to her about how God could fill her life with His Spirit and give her the faith to believe that she would be healed. She looked unbelieving at first; but her situation was desperate and at least what I was saying offered some hope.

A few days later I saw her again and completed a potted "Know Jesus" course. By now she was longing to lay her whole life before the Lord Jesus, and ask Him to fill her with His Spirit. This He graciously did when we prayed and she was filled with praise. I was becoming accustomed to seeing people's lives changed, but something out of the ordinary was happening to Norma.

We didn't pray for physical healing immediately. She knew that Jesus had fulfilled one promise by filling her with His Spirit. She could now believe that He would fulfil another promise and heal her. Both faith and healing are gifts of the Holy Spirit.

When we met again, we prayed that the Lord would heal the disease which was causing paralysis and pain in her body. There was no instant miracle. During the course of the next few months we prayed twice, sometimes three times a week, and I saw the Lord do some remarkable things to Norma during that time.

It seemed that He often performed a kind of physiotherapy releasing the joints from stiffness and pain. First, the neck was freed, then the shoulders and arms, the hips and then the legs. Six months passed — and no sign of a wheelchair being needed! In fact she was not only caring for her family, but still doing a part-time job as well.

I remember laying hands on Norma's back and feeling the locked joints begin to move beneath my hands. On another occasion, one of her fingers was healed. The knuckle joint had disappeared and the finger could not be bent. As we prayed, she began to move the finger. At first there was a slight cracking noise, but this stopped when the joint was completely freed. The finger looked as good as new.

I found it difficult to understand why the healing should take place over a long period. St. Paul talks of gifts of healing, in the plural, and it seemed that the Lord healed in many different ways. Norma's experience taught me many lessons, not least that we need to go on believing in God's power to heal and not give up, just because a miracle does not happen instantly.

At Norma's regular hospital visits, the doctors would check on the rate that paralysis was spreading and her limbs were stiffening. Now they could not understand what was happening; as far as they were concerned it should be impossible for her to walk. In fact, she was walking so well that many of the congregation could not understand why they were being asked to pray for her.

She was asked to spend a few days in hospital, so that tests could be carried out. She didn't want to do this, because she knew the Lord was healing her, but I assured her that there was nothing to fear from God's work being approved by doctors! Norma was subjected to a whole series of examinations, and the doctors could not believe the results of their tests. One morning she was given yet another examination.

"Would you mind telling me what's going on?" Norma asked. "So many doctors have examined me and nobody will tell me why."

"I can't say anything," she was told. "I'm not your doctor. It's amazing, unbelievable. You're a very interesting case."

Fear had begun to stir in Norma. The secrecy of those continual examinations was making her think that perhaps her healing was an illusion, or something temporary, and that the medical evidence did not substantiate it. Her fears were groundless. Her body showed no signs of the serious spinal infection and the rheumatoid arthritis had disappeared. However, the doctors asked Norma's permission to operate on the growth on her spine. She refused. In her heart, Norma knew that the Lord was healing her. She was discharged on the condition that she returned for further examinations.

Norma's healing progressed until there was only one small area of pain towards the base of the spine. This stubbornly refused to move.

During one of the prayer sessions I was led into a new realm of the spiritual life. We were praying about this stubborn point of pain in her back.

"Lord, what do I do now? Why is this pain persisting?" I prayed.

The Lord said to me: "Address the evil."

This came like a thunderbolt from the blue. During my time at college, the devil had been talked out of existence. I had never thought of "addressing" evil. It didn't make sense to talk to Satan, if you didn't believe in him!

My theological training may have discounted the existence of a personal devil, but Jesus believed in his existence and St. Paul tells us that our fight is "against the principalities, against the powers, against the world rulers of this present darkness, against the spiritual hosts of wickedness in the heavenly places" (Eph. 6:12).

"Address the evil," the Lord said. How? I didn't know. I simply said; "I address you power of evil, and in the name of Jesus, I command you to go."

There was an immediate reaction within Norma, as if something had been stirred within her. She was being choked and felt physically sick. This struggle lasted for a few minutes and was followed by peace.

We had entered another dimension of spiritual warfare. When Norma returned to the hospital she was told by the consultant that no operation would be necessary. She was discharged.

It is now three years since I first prayed with Norma. She is fit and shows no sign of ever needing the wheel-chair!

Jesus is concerned to heal the whole person — body, mind and spirit. It is a mistake to imagine that God is only concerned about our spiritual health and it is equally wrong for us to concentrate on physical healing without giving equal importance to the healing of fears, anxieties, doubts, guilt and so on.

During Lent 1971, our understanding of the way in which God wants to heal the lives of His people was increased. We had a course of teaching entitled Jesus Heals.

We were given a prophecy. We had only recently begun to experience the prayer gifts of the Holy Spirit. Words of prophecy were the words that God wanted to speak to us His children — and they were not to be taken lightly. People did not freely speak in the name of the Lord at that time, but when the Holy Spirit did prevail upon someone, we listened.

This prophecy was written down, duplicated and circulated among those who came to the Lent course. The test of prophecy is whether it is true, whether it conforms to the

teaching of Scripture and what fruit it bears in the lives of
those to whom it is addressed. Not that we were so well-
informed at the time. We simply recognised that God had
spoken to our hearts.

These are the words the Lord gave us:

Turn to me and you will be filled with joy and your healing will be assured, for I am the Lord who cares for you
and you are my people whom I shall always love. So come
to me and share in the inheritance that is yours — healing
and wholeness. This is my gift for those who repent, that
they will know that I am their God. They will know that
they can turn to me in their sickness and they will be
healed.

But those who have not turned to me with their whole
heart, they do not know; they do not claim the assurance I
offer them. There is only one way to receive my
gifts — come to me in sorrow for what you have become
and I will make you glad in what you should be — more, I
will pour my gifts into your heart and make you mine
forever.

Rejoice my people, for the day of your deliverance has
come. Turn and be healed, for I would fill you with
myself. My people, I love you. Will you spurn my love?
Will you turn away from I who am your health? My
people, I am your healing and your health, turn to me and
be restored. Be made whole and you will live to my glory
and be happy.

One sentence in particular convinced many people:
"Come to me in sorrow for what you have become and I will
make you glad in what you should be — more, I will pour
my gifts into your heart and make you mine forever."

Week by week the Lord gave us a deeper understanding
of the ways He wanted to bring His healing into our lives.
We began every meeting by giving thanks to Him for the
healing that had taken place since we last met. Not that there
was anything to see. No cripple suddenly danced about the

church in the middle of the meetings. We were just quietly listening to more of what the Lord wanted to do for us, and the level of faith of the congregation as a whole was rising. We were becoming more expectant. The Lord was bringing us from the point of wondering if He would heal, to the point of expecting Him to do so.

Until that Lent many had thought that it was necessary to be desperate about a situation before we could presume to ask God to heal. The Lord showed us that He loved us so much that He was concerned about every detail of our lives. Nothing was unimportant to Him. Nothing too small or insignificant! If we needed healing for anything we could come to Him and ask.

So we found ourselves praising the Lord for healing colds, catarrh, sinus trouble, little aches and pains, stomach disorders, as well as things of greater medical concern.

I learned how, in the Lord, we can resist these common germs. Often, since that time, I have had all the symptoms that herald the arrival of influenza or a heavy cold. If Jesus is Lord of our lives, He is Lord of our bodies. There is no need for our bodies to succumb to these germs. We can praise Him for His victory over them.

When doing this I usually experience a few hours of "battle" going on physically, but the influenza or cold does not develop. I have had only one cold since that Lent, which the Lord used to point out an area of disobedience in my life!

News of the healing that was taking place at St. Hugh's was beginning to reach other churches in the town. I was asked to go to one of these and talk about healing. This was a little shattering. By now I was accustomed to a ready response in people to all the Lord was revealing and doing in our midst, and it seemed incomprehensible that people would want to disbelieve in the Lord's power to heal.

"Why do we need God's healing? We have the National Health Service!" — was the attitude of many.

We welcome the great work of healing through the medical profession. Doctors are co-operating with the healing processes within the Lord's creation. But we were discovering that the Lord was healing the incurables and often saving people from the discomforts of surgery. I have not advised anyone to go against medical advice and have encouraged them to have their healing confirmed by their doctor. God is happy to work alongside, as well as through, the medical profession. It has never made sense to me to say: "You must either go to the Lord or to your doctor." Often people receive very necessary medical treatment and the Lord accelerates the whole healing process while they do so.

I learned an important lesson from that visit to the other church. Healing cannot be isolated from the rest of the Gospel. Jesus promised that He would confirm the Word with signs following. At St. Hugh's we were experiencing the "signs following."

The healings which took place were not only of a physical nature. Pauline was a housewife with a young son, and three daughters: Sue and Elaine were married; Frances was seventeen. Pauline was the only one in her family to attend church. Her husband and daughters showed no interest. Why should they?

"You've been going to church for years, mum — and it doesn't appear to have done you much good," was the girls' attitude.

It is no exaggeration to say that Pauline's life was crippled by fear and guilt. She felt that she was "unclean", that anything she touched became defiled. She was for ever washing her hands and hardly dared touch the vegetables she prepared for her family's meals. One year she arrived at the church on Harvest Thanksgiving day, with her gift, but stopped at the church door.

"I can't offer this gift," she thought to herself. "It is unclean, unholy."

So she turned round and went home, taking her tins with her.

Pauline was constantly afraid that people would notice that she was "unclean", especially the members of her family. Imagine not wanting to touch your own children because you are afraid of contaminating them.

Jesus filled Pauline with His Spirit and healed her of her guilt and fears. She wrote me a letter trying to express the difference in her life.

That other person who was me, no longer exists — is dead, finished, forgotten! IT IS NOT I WHO LIVE BUT CHRIST WHO LIVES WITHIN ME . . .

He accepted me, He welcomed me, He stretched out His arms and took that old sinful person that was me upon the cross that I might die with Him. He gave me new life, His life, His joy, His happiness, His peace.

My heart sings. Jesus takes it all away — all the pain, all the guilt, all the mistakes. How many times I have thought, if only I could have my life over again I wouldn't make the same mistakes.

Because we are what we are, we would probably make exactly the same mistakes all over again.

I have been given a new life, His life within me! How wonderful to be given a second chance and this time I have all His love, pouring into me to help me resist the temptations which I know will still be there!

Already wonderful things have started to happen to me, my life is richer, happier. I seem to be surrounded by love! All the love that He is pouring into my life is overflowing into other people's lives and they are responding to it, warming to it, answering it.

Pauline went on to describe how her relationships with her children were already beginning to change. Whereas before she was too busy and too tired to give them the attention they wanted, now she could relax and give them time. Then she continued:

As I look at the cross, I realise how perfectly this barbaric form of execution fitted into God's purpose. He didn't die on His knees or on the ground in a broken, crumpled heap, but on a cross, raised up above the crowds, His arms outstretched in love as they are today, ready to embrace the whole world.

Even in His agony He interceded on our behalf. "Father, forgive them, for they know not what they do." How can we turn away from such a love?

When I came for healing, I was a little afraid I might be guilty of thinking I was someone special. I can see now how very wrong I was. We are *all* special in God's eyes.

I feel like shouting: "It's true, it's true. Every word you have heard during the past weeks can really happen to you. It's *not* just the new Vicar's funny ideas — but first you must give Jesus your *whole heart*. If you retain, keep back anything, whether from fear or shame or doubt, then you are not offering Him your *whole* heart, your *whole* self. And these are the very things He must take upon the Cross with Him, the sins He died for, if He is to give you new life."

I pray the people of St. Hugh's *will* go on — to happiness, wholeness, forgiveness, and peace. For me the striving is over — I can begin to LIVE.

Praise the Lord, alleluia!!

It didn't take long for Pauline's family to notice the change in her. They had a new mother! Within a few months Elaine, Sue and Frances were Christians filled with the Holy Spirit and praising the Lord.

Pauline's experience is a good example of the power of God's forgiveness, the greatest act of healing in the lives of His people.

Our congregation was steadily increasing as the result of a chain reaction. This was seen in the experience of Pauline and her girls; and the chain didn't end with them. When Frances was filled with the Holy Spirit she was brimming over with joy. She had a boyfriend, Terry, who was horrified at the thought of her going to church; yet he couldn't understand the change that had taken place in her.

She had already joined a prayer group that was not only

concerned with healing, but with bringing people to know
Jesus. The group was praying for Terry because Frances
knew that he would never agree to come to church unless the
Lord used a mighty strong arm!

He was a local "skin-head". When there was trouble or a
rumble among local groups, Terry liked to be in the forefront. One Sunday, Frances persuaded him to come to our
evening service. When he arrived it was obvious that he
hadn't bothered to smarten himself up — a rebel, at sight!

In the church hall after the service, Frances introduced
me to him.

"Well, what did you think of the service?" I asked
politely. I had been preaching about "coming to Jesus."

"It made no impression on *me*," was the confident
reply.

"Dangerous statement." I thought.

The group continued to pray for Terry and on the following Friday morning, I was staggered to see him walking
up the church path, when I arrived to prepare for the Holy
Communion service at seven a.m.! He was alone.

During the General Confession, Terry began to cry. The
rest of the service was punctuated by his sobbing. I went and
sat with him afterwards.

"What have I got to do?" he asked.

"Tell Jesus all about it, and ask Him to forgive you," I
answered.

Terry sank to his knees and poured his heart out to the
Lord, pleading for His forgiveness. I could hardly hear what
he was saying amidst all the tears, but I prayed that the Lord
would forgive him. The tears stopped. Then I laid my hands
on his head. "The Lord has forgiven you, Terry," I said.
Suddenly he stood bolt upright, almost knocking me off bal-
ance.

"I've got it! Thank you very much," he said and strode
out of the church! I was left standing — I hadn't even had
the opportunity to ask the Lord to fill him with the Holy
Spirit!

Terry knew he needed, and had received, the Lord's forgiveness. From that moment his whole way of life changed; he was filled with the Holy Spirit and became another witness to the love of Jesus Christ.

And so the chain reaction continued.

One evening Stella telephoned at about ten o'clock.

"Colin, Lesley is in a bit of a state. Could I bring her to see you please?" she asked.

"Of course," I replied. Lesley was Stella's sixteen year old daughter.

"What's the matter?" I asked, when Lesley arrived.

"I must have this Holy Spirit" she replied. "I've seen it make so many people happy — and receiving the Spirit has made such a difference to mum. I must have the Spirit."

"Why are you so upset?"

"Well," she replied, "earlier this evening I sat down to pray and begged the Spirit to come to me, and nothing happened. For two hours I pleaded and still nothing."

"When you prayed, what did you say?" I asked.

"I said: 'Come to me Lord. Come to me. Please come to me. Come to me.' But nothing happened. He seems so far away from me."

"I'm not surprised," I said. I held my two hands up, with about a foot's distance between them. I moved the left hand slightly. "That's you," I said to Lesley. Then I moved the right hand slightly. "That's Jesus."

"Jesus isn't far away from you; just one step. You are standing there saying 'Jesus, Jesus, come to me,' and Jesus is standing before you saying, 'Lesley, Lesley, come to me.' Someone has to give way." Lesley smiled.

I went on to explain how we need to come to Jesus, not expect Him to come to us. This meant giving Him our lives. I suggested to Lesley that she went home and prepared to give her life to the Lord.

We arranged to meet for prayer three or four days later; Lesley gave her life to Jesus and was filled with the Holy Spirit. I left her quietly praising the Lord in tongues.

I was growing accustomed to a new type of ministry, as

well as a new way of life, and was discovering that the Holy
Spirit is full of surprises in the way He chooses to work. The
needs of each person are different. Those who minister in
the power of the Holy Spirit must listen to Him in every
situation and learn the lessons that He teaches in each experience.

"Lord, what on earth are you doing?" I thought. "Not
yet; she doesn't understand what it's all about."

The Lord was disrupting our nice, neat, orderly way of
going about things! During the closing prayers of the first
session of a "Know Jesus" group, Janet had been filled with
the Holy Spirit.

When I talked to her after the meeting she looked so full
of fear and anguish that I doubted whether she had really
been baptised in the Holy Spirit. But obviously the Lord
knew what He was doing.

For several days, I had to spend some time listening to
Janet, as she poured out the deep resentments, hatred and
bitterness that had been stored up within her. On each
occasion, more of the Spirit seemed to be released in her.
Over a period of about three weeks, she began to show the
joy, the love, the peace, that I had grown accustomed to
seeing in those newly baptised in the Holy Spirit.

God was doing an important work of healing in Janet.
The Holy Spirit had filled her and was pushing to the surface
all the rubbish hidden deep within her, rubbish that would
never have been uncovered by a simple act of repentance.

Not everybody is like Janet. Some people have difficulty
in accepting that Jesus has baptised them in the Holy
Spirit.

Stuart was an eighteen-year-old Baptist. He loved Jesus
and had a deep faith in Him, but he recognised a lack of
power in his Christian life. At the end of a "Know Jesus"
group, we prayed together. He offered his life totally, and
asked to be filled with the Holy Spirit. As he did not belong
to our Church, I hardly saw anything of him until about
three months later.

"Can I come and see you as soon as possible, please?"

Stuart's voice sounded troubled on the telephone. The following day, when he walked into my study, he obviously was troubled; in fact, he didn't look at all like the calm Stuart I had known.

"I've never felt so miserable," he told me. That was easy to believe from his appearance.

"What's the trouble?" I asked.

"It all began when I asked you to pray with me to be baptised with the Holy Spirit," replied Stuart.

"What happened then?"

"Nothing — that's the problem — nothing happened."

Stuart is not a great talker, but for about twenty minutes, I sat and listened while he told me of the misery of the last three months. He had felt rejected by God and had come to the conclusion that Jesus had refused to baptise him with the Spirit. He had spent long hours in prayer, pleading with God to fill him. He gave up hope of finding the answer at home. So he decided to take what little money he had, leave home, and trust God for everything. Maybe He would answer then.

On the first night, God made Stuart deeply aware of His love for him. Trying to settle down to sleep in a field about fifteen miles from Luton, was not what the Lord wanted!

"He spoke to me and told me to come and see you," said Stuart. "So here I am."

"What made you think that nothing happened when we prayed?" I asked.

"I didn't have an experience or speak in tongues."

"Well Stuart, I am not going to pray with you again to be filled with the Spirit. You opened your life to the Lord, and we prayed in faith that He would baptise you with His Spirit. You did pray in faith, didn't you?"

"Yes."

"We are told in the Scriptures," I continued, "that when any two agree their prayer will be granted. So as far as I am concerned you were baptised in the Holy Spirit three months ago."

Stuart said nothing. He still looked glum.

"The only problem is that you have not accepted the gift the Lord has given you."

Signs of hope could be seen in his face.

"You love the Lord, don't you Stuart?"

"Yes."

"Do you trust the Lord?"

"Yes."

'Are you prepared to trust Him now?"

A slight pause, then he answered with a tentative "Yes".

"Right," I said. "I am going to pray now and I want you to pray with me. I am not going to ask the Lord to fill you with His Spirit; He has already done that. Instead we are going to praise the Lord together — in tongues!"

Stuart looked far from certain.

"Trust the Lord," I said. "Open your mouth, begin to speak, and trust the Lord to give you the words."

I began to pray. About twenty seconds later both of us were praising the Lord in tongues together!

When Stuart left the house a few minutes later, his feet were hardly touching the ground. He was flooded with the love and joy of Jesus as he accepted in his heart that the Lord had fulfilled His promise. He has continued to grow in the life of the Spirit ever since.

There are occasions when it is not right to pray with people.

Phillip was twenty, and an ardent young Christian. He was always devising schemes, arranging outings for pensioners, organising sponsored walks and other events for charity. Most things went well; sometimes his schemes backfired and occasionally he was the despair of the local clergy. He would visit them regularly, hoping to encourage them to support his latest venture.

When we prayed, Phillip opened his life to the Lord. When it came to my turn to pray for him, I couldn't. I asked him to sit down.

"Phillip, something is wrong. I can't pray for you," I said.

"You're absolutely right," he replied and immediately fell on his knees again.

"Lord," he prayed, "I have offered you my life — the life that everybody else sees, the popular Phillip: but You know that is not the real me."

He went on to give the Lord the real Phillip that lay beneath that brash exterior. Then we prayed. It was the real Phillip, whom Jesus wanted to fill with His Holy Spirit.

We have realised that God wants to baptise every one of His people in the Holy Spirit. All Christians need this release of His love and power and joy and peace, to enable them to live fruitful and effective lives as members of the Body of Christ in the world.

John the Baptist said of Jesus: "I have baptised you with water; but He will baptise you with the Holy Spirit" (Mark 1: 8). When Jesus baptises a person in His Holy Spirit, the Son of God touches his life personally. Only by coming to Jesus can that promise be fulfilled. If we have opened our hearts to Him, we can accept confidently that He has honoured His promise and a new life in the Spirit will begin.

6 Oppression and Praise

"FELLOWSHIP IN THE Holy Spirit" was the theme of an international conference organised by the Fountain Trust, in July 1971. It sounded interesting, although until that time none of us at St. Hugh's knew anything about what is commonly known as the "charismatic movement". We were not conscious of being part of any movement, we had simply been seeking the power of God.

For the past year I had been too busy trying to keep up with all the developments in our church to think very much about what was happening in the church throughout the world!

"What on earth have I let myself in for?" — was my reaction on the first evening. Somebody had begun the proceedings by asking us to sing choruses! "Just as well the others at St. Hugh's can't see me now," I thought. I had been brought up to believe it was impossible to sink any lower than singing evangelical choruses!

Then I began to grow alarmed! I was enjoying them! In fact I felt frustrated because I didn't know the words of those not in the book. There was a simplicity about these songs that was lovely. They were expressing truths about God with a directness that is to be found in very few poetic hymns!

That conference taught me a great deal. It was good to feel at one in the Spirit with everybody I spoke to, and it was surprising to me that church background and denominationalism were irrelevant. It was wonderful to hear of the way God was renewing His church all over the world, by the power of the Holy Spirit. I was introduced to singing in the Spirit. Hundreds of voices blended harmoniously as we allowed the Spirit to give us tunes, as well as words, to praise our Heavenly Father. The most beautiful sound I had ever heard.

At Guildford, where the conference took place, I learned that the Lord had the power to meet any need in the lives of His children. On arriving home from the conference, something strange happened. About five months previously, I had lost a bunch of keys, including my car key. They were nowhere to be found, so I shared Caroline's. My keys were not in the pockets, or the lining of my anorak; I had searched thoroughly on more than one occasion.

I needed to use the car urgently. My wife was out and her keys nowhere to be found! What should I do? Sit down and pray of course!

I went into my study and prayed: "Lord, please lead me to where Caroline's keys are," fully expecting Him to put into my mind where they were. Instead, nothing! Absolutely nothing!

"Lord, you know I need those keys." Still nothing.

"Well, Lord, I'm going out to the car and somehow I trust you to start it." I put on my anorak, shoved my hands into the pockets, as I usually did, and found that my left hand was clenching a bunch of keys! I took them out of my pocket.

They were not my wife's keys, but the bunch I had lost five months previously! I stood in the hall, completely dumbfounded. That anorak had been with me at Guildford and I knew those keys were not in the pocket!

Later, I confirmed that neither Caroline, nor any of the children had seen them!

That is the sort of experience that many people will want to explain away. Since that time the Lord has given many other signs of His love whenever there has been a real need.

Why not, if He loves us?

Caroline didn't know what to make of such things; she was perplexed enough already. It seemed that her husband had changed so much and yet she was completely unchanged. If anything, she resented the changes that He had caused in me. Marrying a clergyman was bad enough, but to find yourself involved in the miraculous was ridiculous!

She found it difficult enough to believe in the Lord, without being asked to believe in miracles! And there were certain very human problems. To Caroline my hands had become something sacred. They were used by the Lord to heal, to fill people with His Spirit. She felt that it was wrong to expect those same hands to touch her in a loving and affectionate way. They belonged to the Lord, not to her. In fact, Colin belonged to the Lord, not to her.

Choruses were introduced in the Bible study groups. The first reaction of others was similar to mine; but people soon began to value them as a great vehicle of praise. They helped us to express the praise God had put into our hearts.

There was no opposition in the church to the developments that were taking place. Why should there be, when so many wonderful things were happening as a result? A few members chose to stand on the sidelines and observe what was going on; some didn't want to commit their lives completely to the Lord. They had been used to a certain way of church life for many years and couldn't see any need to change. This made us sad, but they were people we all respected and no pressure was put on them to be filled with the Spirit.

In fact, it is very difficult to think of any who did not become involved in some way, in the developments that were taking place. For nearly everyone in the whole church family was a member of a prayer and healing group, and virtually everyone accepted the invitation to come to a "Know Jesus" course.

It was not until September 1971, that the phrase "baptism in the Holy Spirit" was mentioned from the pulpit — fifteen

months after the first "Know Jesus" group began. I was not
afraid to use the term, but it would have been meaningless
or confusing to many if I had. By then two-thirds of the
congregation had come into this experience and there was so
much talk generally between members of the church family
about the activity of the Holy Spirit in their lives, that no
one commented when "baptism in the Holy Spirit" was
eventually used in sermons.

Although we were spared human opposition, someone
else was becoming extremely concerned about all that was
happening at St. Hugh's. Call him the enemy, Satan, the ac-
cuser, or what you will, he was beginning to rear his head. In
fact, we came to know him as "Big Boots" because he was
always trying to get his foot into whatever was going on.

I have already described my first encounter with the
enemy, when Norma was being healed. I kept very quiet
about it at the time; it would not have been helpful to share
it with others. But Satan does not like being disturbed, and
he was certainly not pleased with all these people at St.
Hugh's praising the Lord!

In October I went for my annual retreat, expecting to
have a great time spiritually. Instead I felt dreadful. I am not
prone to periods of depression, but that week everything
seemed as black as it could be.

I did all the right things; I confessed to the Lord, read the
Bible as much as possible, tried to pray and praise; but there
was this heaviness. One thought kept coming into my mind:
"All those times when you prayed with Norma, why didn't
you discern that there was a problem of evil? You can't
discern spirits can you? Ha! Ha!" It was as if I was being
jeered at, and that made matters worse.

I knew these were lying thoughts that were being pushed
at me. The Lord had revealed the problem and He had dealt
with it. I knew He had forgiven any failure on my part to
listen to what He was saying; yet the heaviness continued for
three days. One of the main purposes of a retreat is to have
time to pray and that was what I found so desperately
difficult.

I went to sleep on the Wednesday night exhausted by the battle that was going on within me, hoping that I would feel different in the morning. But no, there was the same heaviness, the same blackness. I went down to the chapel and sat through Matins, unable to participate properly. There was a brief interval before Holy Communion.

"This is ridiculous!" I thought. "I can't go on like this."

I knelt down. "Lord, make this a day of praise for you."

I cannot adequately describe the next half hour of my life, while that service was taking place. If it is possible for a human being to go to heaven, while still in the body, then I went there. The heaviness and darkness completely lifted. I was in the midst of glory, surrounded by praise. I was there before the Lord, worshipping and adoring Him.

It is impossible to describe this experience adequately. My face felt as if it was burning. When praising the Lord, it is not an uncommon experience to be "aglow with the Spirit," but this was much more intense. At the end of the service I felt as if I had been scorched by a hot sun all day long!

Somebody sitting near me in the chapel later told me that it was obvious that something truly wonderful was happening to me. Judging from the strange looks I was getting during breakfast, I guess my face must have appeared sunburnt. If heaven is as wonderful as that, then I thank God with all my heart that He has saved me from death, through Jesus, that He has given me eternal life and promised me a place in glory with Him for ever!

When I returned home on the Friday, the gloom of the first few days had been completely dispelled by the praise of the last day. The Bible study group met that evening and I felt moved to share with them what had happened on the retreat — the gloom, the despair, the praise and the glory.

The reaction of everyone surprised me! They had all been going through an attack of oppression from the enemy. Some had even felt tempted to chuck the whole business in — why be a Christian at all? A real fight had been going on.

At various times on the Thursday, every member of the group had been delivered by the Lord in one way or another. The words which He taught us to pray "deliver us from evil", meant much more to us after that.

We praised the Lord that night for the victory He had won in our lives. As a result of the last few days, I had been humbled and broken before the Lord in a deeper way, and He had raised me to new heights of praise. What glory awaits all those who love Him.

From that time our corporate life, as well as our individual lives, began to alter. One of the first visible changes affected our worship.

Our main service had always been the Parish Communion at nine thirty on Sunday morning. A greater sense of worship and praise was growing at this, although the form of the service remained unchanged. Nor did we have any desire to alter it. We were conscious that the Lord wanted the whole church to remain united and that unity was expressed in the Parish Communion. We must love the brethren whose hearts had not yet been filled to overflowing with love and praise for the Lord. They were just as much part of the family as those who had come into the experience of being baptised in the Holy Spirit.

Every Sunday evening we had the Anglican service of Evensong. This is not a form of worship that appeals to new Christians of whom we had many. Attendance was very small — a dozen was a crowd. Those who regularly came often remarked: "If only more people would come in the evening."

For months at staff meetings we had been saying, "We must do something about Evensong." But there were so many other things to do.

We needed a form of service in which people could feel free to express the praise in their hearts. The Church Council agreed that "Evening Praise" should begin. We talked about this with the Evensong congregation, and nobody raised any objections.

Thirty-six people arrived for the first Evening Praise. Instead of leaving only the preaching open to the Lord, the entire service was unstructured, so that we could allow the Holy Spirit to lead us.

Needless to say, there was plenty of praise; but there was also opportunity for quiet meditation after the Bible readings. The sermons at Parish Communion were usually short, because of the number of young children present. At Evening Praise there was opportunity to expand our meditation on the Scriptures — and we were beginning to recognise our need for more teaching and revelation through the Word of God.

After four weeks the size of the evening congregation had risen to almost eighty and within six months to about one hundred and fifty.

Each week was different. Sometimes there seemed to be a great emphasis on praise and joy; at other times the service was very quiet. The Lord dealt lovingly with His children every week. God was at work among us.

Evening Praise lasted at least an hour and a half, sometimes two hours. Yet the children loved to come; they enjoyed praising the Lord, particularly in the free time of worship that often ended the service. Choruses were coming into their own and the children (young and old!) loved them.

But then the Lord was beginning to do some very wonderful things in the lives of our children . . .

7 Even Our Children

"COULD YOU COME and lay hands on him please?" Rosemary asked.

Christopher, her thirteen-year-old son was in bed with bronchitis and although the doctor had been treating him, he didn't appear to be making any progress.

"I'll be there later this morning," I replied.

Rosemary and her husband Cliff had been amongst the first to be baptised in the Holy Spirit at St. Hugh's. It was nearly lunchtime when I arrived at their home. It was my usual practice now to pray in tongues when on my way to visit someone. I was more open to the leading of the Holy Spirit when I had been allowing Him to pray in me.

As I went up to Chris's room the Lord told me to talk to him about the Holy Spirit. It had never occurred to any of us that the Lord wanted to fill children with the Spirit! They weren't old enough!

I asked Rosemary to wait downstairs.

"Chris, I want to talk to you about the Holy Spirit," I began. I went on to explain very briefly and simply how Jesus wanted to come into his life and fill him with the Spirit.

"Whether you want Jesus or not, is entirely up to you. You must decide." I said.

"I do," replied Christopher. "I can see what a difference He has made to Mum and Dad."

"I had better say something about tongues," I thought

59

— after all you never know what might happen once the Lord is allowed freedom to work.

I explained that I might speak in tongues and told Christopher not to be frightened if he felt the urge to do the same. He said a very simple prayer, asking Jesus to be Lord in his life, and I laid hands on him praying that Jesus would fill him with the Holy Spirit. "Now Chris, I want you to pray out loud, and let the Holy Spirit give you the words to say."

He began to pray a beautiful prayer about the fountains of God's glory, hardly the kind you would expect from a thirteen-year-old boy! It was full of love and praise and was an obvious sign that the Lord was doing something very important in young Christopher.

I explained to Rosemary and Cliff what had happened, wondering what their reaction would be. They were delighted! Together we asked the Lord to heal Christopher's bronchitis. After praying in English I laid hands over his chest and prayed in tongues. Chris looked much better; I left, praising the Lord.

Soon after I had gone, he got up and spent the remainder of the day downstairs. Later that afternoon he asked Rosemary: "Did you understand what Colin was saying when he spoke in tongues?"

"No," replied Rosemary.

"I did," said Christopher. "The Lord was speaking to me. He kept on saying 'Christopher, Christopher, come to me. I am the living Christ.' He said it over and over again until I said, 'Yes, Lord, I come.' Then He healed me."

Later that evening, Christopher praised the Lord in tongues for the first time. For years Christopher had suffered from asthma, but since that time he has never suffered an asthmatic attack.

Some of the healings the Lord performs in the lives of people are personal signs to them of His love. There are other occasions when the Lord is doing something in the life of one person that needs to be shared with others, because of the bearing it could have on their lives. Christopher's experience was just such a case.

It underlined the truth that we were not to expect Jesus to
come to us — we were to come to Him. We were made to
consider also the whole position of the children in our
church family. It so happened that our annual confirmation
service was only about three weeks away. Among the candidates was a group of fifteen children, between the ages of ten
and fifteen. David, who had replaced Michael on the parish
staff, was in charge of their preparation class.

"David, I think the Lord wants to baptise these children
in the Holy Spirit when they are confirmed," I said. Because
he had only recently come into this experience himself, I
went to one of the preparation classes to talk to them.

On the evening prior to the confirmation service all the
candidates, children and adults, were in church to go
through the form of service. I said to them: "Just before the
Bishop lays his hands on your head say quietly 'Lord, fill me
with your Holy Spirit *NOW*, please!' and expect Jesus to do
precisely that. When you go back to your seat, begin to
praise the Lord that He has fulfilled His promise."

There was a great air of expectancy on the morning of the
confirmation. Everybody had been asked to come twenty
minutes earlier than usual, to have a time of prayer before
the service began. We prayed that we would see the Spirit
move in the lives of those who were to be confirmed, including the children.

They had obviously listened to what I had said the evening before. The Lord not only filled them with His Spirit,
but when they went back to their places they were speaking
in tongues, interpreting and prophesying quietly among
themselves!

Those children continued to meet as a prayer group and I
shall always remember the first time I joined them.

All of them were sitting around the lounge of David's
house. They first expressed their own needs: a sniffle here, a
sore throat there — nothing very serious. They prayed for
one another and thanked the Lord for His healing. Then
they prayed for others. On that occasion they prayed for
three people, all of whom were healed that night, including

someone with a serious mental condition. God certainly hears the prayers of His young children.

One member of the group, Debbie, did have something more seriously wrong with her. She had been born deaf in one ear. The group undertook to pray for her. A little while later she received the laying on of hands and imagine her delight when she could put the telephone to her "deaf" ear and hear!

Jesus said: "Except you become as little children ...". There is a beautiful simplicity in the faith of children. When they believe, they believe. There are few "ifs" and "buts".

The experience of that group of youngsters made us see that children could be filled with love and praise for the Lord. However, we realised that the last thing we must do was to persuade them to be filled with the Spirit. Each would come to the Lord at the right time.

One Sunday, when I arrived home after the evening service, Claire and Clive had just gone to bed. Claire was then six years old and Clive, four.

"Go up and kiss the children goodnight," Caroline called out as I came in.

As I entered the bedroom the two children shared, I heard Clive ask: "Where is Jesus?"

"He's alive inside us. Didn't you know that, silly?" Claire answered. Just like an elder sister! "That's right isn't it Dad?" she asked as I walked up to her bed.

"Yes, that's right," I said.

"Can Jesus live in me?" asked Claire.

"Yes, He can live in anyone who wants Him."

"How?"

Ah! Now I knew the answer!

"Tell the Lord you want to give Him your life and ask Him to come and live in you," I said.

Immediately, Claire knelt on top of her bed, closed her eyes and put her hands together, in good Sunday School style. "Please Jesus, come and live in me," she prayed.

She looked happy.

"I want you to pray again," I told her; "this time, let Jesus give you the words to say."

She prayed for all the people in the world who do not know the Lord, that they might come to see His glory. Hardly the prayer of a six-year-old.

Dad was happy! — and I expect our heavenly Father was smiling too!

"Now then, come along, its time you tucked down and went to sleep." I said to them both.

"Wait a minute, Daddy, I haven't said my other prayer," protested Claire.

"What other prayer?"

She began to speak in tongues! I was amazed. It was possible that Claire had heard some conversation about this gift of the Spirit, but as far as I could remember she had never heard anybody speak in tongues. I may have done so, when praying with her to be healed at some time. I couldn't recall doing so and certainly never expected to hear her speak in tongues at that time!

The Lord gave me an interpretation about the children of God rejoicing in Him, and Dad went downstairs very happy!

"I wonder what Caroline will make of this?" I thought.

The children of our church families seemed to be growing up into a natural relationship with the Lord, and were often a source of inspiration to us all. They were surrounded by an atmosphere of faith and praise. Their parents had been drawn into a real relationship with Jesus, so it was natural for them to want their children to share in the life of the Spirit.

Andrea, our youngest child, spoke in tongues when she was just three. To be more precise: she sang in tongues. She displays a natural love for the Lord and often goes around the house singing beautiful little Jesus songs. Some of these she has heard before: others are obviously inspired by the Spirit and given to her.

Andy was sitting in the back of our car while Caroline

was driving, deep in conversation with a friend. They were suddenly aware that she was no longer singing in English; she was singing in tongues, quite oblivious to everyone and everything around her as she praised the Lord.

If adults, with their greater command of the English language run out of vocabulary when praising God, why shouldn't a three-year-old child?

One of our greatest little witnesses to the Lord's love, is young Lorraine. She is a spinabifida child whose parents, John and Jean, were converted when she was six. Even at that age she would tell people unashamedly "Jesus is looking after me". When Lorraine talks of her experience of the Lord in prayer, nobody could doubt the reality of her relationship with Him.

At the end of one Good Friday service, the Lord indicated that He wanted us to pray with her. The following morning, John and Jean were woken by her shouting from her bedroom: "Mummy, Mummy, I've got fat legs." Her legs, which had been like two matchsticks, had begun to take shape. Although the Lord has done a great deal of healing in her life, there is still a long way to go before she is completely healed.

With all the talk about the healing power of Christ, our children accepted Him naturally as the source of healing. It became common for parents to pray with their children, and often there was no need to send for a doctor. If they felt unwell, my own children would come and say: "Dad, please ask Jesus to make me feel better."

One Sunday morning a nine-year-old girl called Clare (not our daughter) came up to me before Parish Communion.

"Colin, I've got hay-fever. Would you pray with me after the service please?" she said.

"Yes, of course I will. You expect Jesus to make you better and He will," I replied.

Clare patiently waited while I talked to people at Parish Breakfast. She was never far away from me, as if to say: "You haven't forgotten have you?"

"Come along, Clare. Let's go into the church and pray."

"When blind Bartimeus came to Jesus to be healed He said to him: 'What do you want me to do for you?' Jesus knew what Bartimeus needed — it was obvious. But did he have the faith to ask Jesus to heal his eyes? He answered: 'Master, I want my sight back!' Now Clare, you be like Bartimeus; tell Jesus what you want Him to do for you."

Clare prayed a simple prayer, asking the Lord to take away her hay-fever, from which she was in some discomfort. We prayed together, asking the Lord to heal her.

Clare sniffed. All seemed clear. She sniffed again – all was clear! "Thank you Jesus," she said.

Even with children, my job was to pray with them, not do the praying for them!

Perhaps the most remarkable healing that took place in the life of a child, concerned David. He was two years old, and almost a human vegetable; he could not stand or walk. He sat on the floor all day long, with a totally blank expression on his face, unable to hear and hardly able to see. The amount of brain damage left no hope of David ever improving through medical treatment.

His family had only just moved into the district, when Shirley, his mother, fell into conversation with two other housewives who live in the same street, Maggie and Tina, both members of St. Hugh's.

When Shirley told them about David they said that they would pray for him at their healing group, which happened to meet that evening. Immediately David began to change. Within two weeks, he was not only standing, he was running! And he could hear! And he was beginning to talk! And that blank expression had gone! Instead he was laughing and even singing.

Shirley was accused of bringing the wrong child when she next visited the clinic. "That can't possibly be the child referred to in these notes," she was told. The health visitor said that in all her experience she had never known any child to be healed of such advanced brain damage. When you know Jesus, anything is possible.

It was good that Maggie should have been one of those involved in David's healing. She was a trained nurse and when she first came to St. Hugh's she could accept everything — except the Lord's healing. Her medical training denied that such things could happen. However, the Lord gave Maggie the faith to trust Him even for healing, once she was baptised in the Holy Spirit.

8 Coming and Going

"PRAISE THE LORD, He has fulfilled His words of prophecy tonight." Tears were streaming down the old man's face as he spoke.

"What do you mean?" I asked.

"Forty years ago," he answered, "I was a founder member of this church — one of the first to be baptised in the Holy Spirit in this town. There was only a small group of us then and none of the other churches wanted anything to do with us. When we met together, we prayed that the Lord would bring revival to His church in this town."

The old man could hardly continue speaking, he was so overcome with emotion.

"One day the Lord gave us a prophecy. He told us that the Spirit would move in Luton from the circumference to the centre and from the centre to the circumference. For forty years I have been praying that I would live to see the Lord fulfil that prophecy — and He has tonight."

It happens that the Pentecostal church is right in the centre of the town, and St. Hugh's is on the very circumference!

I was deeply moved and thankful. That man and his friends (he was the only one still living of that original group) had believed what God had promised. I began to realise that what was happening at St. Hugh's was based upon forty years of faithful prayer.

I had been speaking at The Assemblies of God Pentecostal

Church and had explained briefly how the Spirit was moving in our church. In particular I had spoken about the way the Lord wanted to continually fill the lives of His children with His Holy Spirit. I felt that He was going to pour a fresh anointing on that gathering, when the sermon ended.

In the silence that followed we laid our lives open to the Lord, and prayed that the Holy Spirit would descend on us all. He did. Suddenly there was a great spontaneous burst of praise. The silence was broken by everyone praising the Lord at precisely the same moment.

Soon after my arrival in Luton I met Colin, the pastor of that church, when he and Wynn, the Elim Pentecostal pastor, were speaking about healing at a ministers' fraternal. After the meeting I introduced myself to them and told them of my involvement in the healing ministry.

"Do you come from an evangelical background?" one of them asked me, predictably perhaps.

"No," I replied, "I'm a Pentecostal Anglican!"

Wynn and Colin looked at one another, suspicion written all over their faces.

They began to question me closely about my experience of being baptised in the Holy Spirit. We ended our conversation with hearty handshakes and several acclamations of "Praise the Lord". I had two new and very good friends.

About a year later a group of ministers began to meet in our vicarage to study the Bible and pray in the Spirit together. This group still meets every fortnight and I have valued tremendously the fellowship that we have experienced together. Both Colin and Wynn were members of this group from the beginning and I am deeply indebted to them for all I have learned from their great understanding of the Scriptures and their experiences of life "in the Spirit".

They had another great virtue — they both shared my love for cricket. Many are the games we have played together and in opposition.

"When it comes to unity, Wynn, we had better stick to the

Holy Spirit, not the cricket field!" He used to get very excited if St. Hugh's showed signs of beating Elim in one of our evening *friendly* matches!

When Wynn and I shared the platform at a Council of Churches meeting on "Healing", it surprised many that a Pentecostal and an Anglican could speak about anything with such agreement and concord.

At the Guildford Conference it became apparent that the Holy Spirit was moving all over the world, bringing renewed power into the lives of Christians of just about every denomination. I realised that we at St. Hugh's would benefit from receiving teaching from others who had longer experience of this life "in the Spirit".

We had booked the diocesan Retreat House in St. Albans for a weekend in January 1972. I wrote to Michael Harper and asked him to lead the weekend for us, enclosing some details about St. Hugh's.

Michael telephoned me a few days later to say that he was unable to come. I was surprised that he seemed excited about the way things were developing in our church and asked if someone could visit the parish to prepare a report for the Fountain Trust magazine *Renewal*.

"Well yes, I suppose so," I answered. I must have sounded absolutely bewildered. I simply could not understand why such interest should be taken in us.

It was only when Eric Meyer visited the parish for the Fountain Trust that I discovered that, while the Lord was blessing many individuals and groups of people both inside and outside the established churches, it was still rare for a whole church to come alive in the Spirit. I had assumed that this was a natural thing to happen.

Eric was concerned to know if what was happening was a genuine work of the Holy Spirit. He questioned me about every aspect of our church life, and also had a meeting with a group of lay people, without me being present.

When the article appeared in *Renewal* the following February it had a considerable influence on our parish life. People began to visit us from all over the place, sometimes undertaking journeys of up to fifty miles in each direction, just to be present at one of our services.

We recognised that we must be very firm and not encourage anybody to leave their own churches to come and join St. Hugh's. God wants to renew the whole of His church, not just an isolated one here and there. We were quite happy for people to come and have fellowship with us, for obviously many of our visitors were starved of fellowship in the Spirit in their own churches.

We began an open prayer meeting in the vicarage every Friday night, when as many as sixty people crammed into our lounge. These were times of great rejoicing in the Lord, and the prayer would continue for three hours or more.

It was ridiculous; praying for three hours! Why only a few months before many of us had found it difficult to pray for three minutes! Now it was a joy to be together in the Lord, even if it was a crush.

When the Holy Spirit is allowed to pray in us, prayer ceases to be the drudge it has often been before.

One day a young housewife came to see me, looking very upset. She had only been coming to St. Hugh's for a couple of weeks.

"Everybody around me in church seems to be able to pray. They're not just pretending: they are really praying. But I can't, I'm the only one not praying!" she sobbed. "I've tried at home too. If I sit down and try to concentrate for five minutes even, my mind wanders all over the place. I just cannot pray."

I waited for the tears to subside. Then I told her briefly that the others were able to pray because Jesus had filled their lives with His Spirit. "He wants to fill you, too," I said.

There was a longing for Jesus in her eyes.

"Let's pray together before you go home," I suggested.

Jesus baptised her with His Spirit and answered the longing in her heart.

Two days later she came bursting into my study. "It's wonderful! It's wonderful! I can't stop praying. I sit down; I start to pray and I have to make myself stop to prepare my husband's dinner."

"Well, don't bother to stop," I said. "Keep on praying while you're cooking."

When we do things in our own strength they are difficult, but when the Lord does them in us, then it is wonderful!

The first visiting speaker at St. Hugh's was David Smith, who came instead of Michael Harper to lead our retreat weekend. Imagine the joy during one of the sessions when suddenly Ray began to praise the Lord aloud in tongues. Ray had been one of the churchwardens when I arrived at St. Hugh's, and he had been the one person who had dropped out of the first "Know Jesus" group.

David was soon followed by another visitor, Dr. Richard Carter, an American evangelist with a Southern Baptist background. You could hardly imagine anyone more opposite to a bunch of Anglicans with a catholic tradition. However, the three nights when he spoke and ministered were times of great sharing together in the Spirit.

Dick Carter opened up for us further the use of the spiritual gifts. In particular we saw in his ministry the word of knowledge and the word of wisdom being manifested, as he prayed with people individually.

On the first evening a group of nurses was sitting in the front row. Dick went straight up to one of them and said quietly to her, "It's time your rebellion against the Lord stopped."

The girl looked stunned. The Lord had spoken precisely the right words to her through Dick. She was feeling completely rebellious and was there only because she had been dragged along by a group of friends.

A few days later that girl was filled with the Holy Spirit and was given a great love for Jesus. Her days of rebellion were over.

Dick's ministry was very different from anything we had encountered before; but we were learning something of the diversity of the Holy Spirit. The meetings at which he ministered were attended by many people from local Pentecostal and other churches, which were beginning to sit up and take notice of the way the Spirit was moving at St. Hugh's. We found this natural unity with our Spirit-filled brethren right there in our own church building.

More people were also coming from other churches to our "Know Jesus" groups — Roman Catholics, Baptists, Congregationalists, Anglicans, Methodists, even a few from the Brethren, who openly preach against baptism in the Holy Spirit. Having been filled with the Spirit these Christian brothers and sisters would go back to their churches with our blessing. Many still come for fellowship with us occasionally, and it has been thrilling to hear how the blessing of the Holy Spirit has spread within their churches.

As the months passed, suspicion amongst other Anglican clergy in Luton became less noticeable and several asked if they could come to "Know Jesus" groups. I always find it a very humbling experience praying with brother clergy, as they lay their lives and ministries before the Lord and ask for the release of the power of the Holy Spirit.

During the international conference, I absconded for half a day to play cricket! The diocesan cricket team had an important cup match at Epsom, not far from Guildford. Should anyone think this was putting the things of the flesh before the things of the Spirit, I will rapidly relate how the Lord used it for His purpose!

Frank was playing for the opposing side. We had been at college together and he was then rector of a church near Brighton. During the tea interval he asked me why I was at Guildford and the conversation drifted on to what was happening at St. Hugh's.

"I am really interested in this," Frank said. "I would like to know much more."

However I had to leave before the end of the match, as I did not want to miss the evening service of the conference in Guildford Cathedral. (My heart was in the right place after all!).

A few weeks later I received a telephone call from Frank.

"Colin, could we meet and talk more about this business of the Holy Spirit?"

It was arranged that I should go to Brighton for a day to talk to Frank. Our time together ended with him laying his life before the Lord and asking to be baptised in the Holy Spirit. He found a new conviction and authority in his ministry. But it was not easy to know how to share this experience with others in his church. Some teenagers were hungry for reality in their Christian lives; so Frank asked me to revisit the parish some months later to lead a youth weekend.

A group of our young people came with me, including Christopher (who was healed of bronchitis), and Terry — only a six week old Christian then!

When we arrived in the church hall, all the youngsters were sitting around waiting, looking miserable. They must have wondered what had hit them as we began to sing choruses together. I thought of the shock I had received almost a year before when I was expected to sing to them for the first time! However, after a few spiritual songs, they all looked happier and much more relaxed.

God began to show those young people the kind of Christian life He wanted them to have, and on the Saturday evening we prayed with nearly thirty of them, asking Jesus to fill them with the Holy Spirit.

When it came to the Sunday session there were not only young people present, but a group of parents as well.

"We had to come and find out what this wonderful thing is that has happened to our children," one parent told me.

"It's amazing — he's so different," a perplexed mother said.

After a short talk, it seemed right to have an informal time together. I suggested that the parents speak to the young members of the team I had brought with me.

Jesus said, "You shall receive power when the Holy Spirit has come upon you and you shall be my witnesses..." (Acts 1: 8). I stood and watched with praise in my heart. Clusters of adults were gathered around the members of our team, while these youngsters told them about Jesus and the Holy Spirit. Many of those parents had been regular church members for as long as they could remember; yet our young people were talking about a relationship with God that was deeper than anything they had known.

"Jesus is so wonderful," I overheard Christopher say with simplicity.

"Jesus will really forgive all your sins and give you a new life," Terry said with conviction. You only had to look at Frances to see that she was radiant with the Spirit.

The afternoon session was due to end in time for people to go to the evening service. Instead Frank went off to officiate and left us to continue with the conference. We ended with a lovely time of praise, during which we ministered personally to several of the parents.

I was whacked! A four-hour drive home, and the others sang all the way! Even when you're tired it is very difficult not to sing, if there is so much praise for the Lord in your heart!

I was used to introducing people gently to the baptism in the Holy Spirit, giving them time to prepare an offering of their lives and praying with each one in a personal way. When asked to lead a "New Life" conference at Southport, I found myself in a very different situation. I felt on the second evening that the Lord was wanting some people to come forward for prayer. My reaction only a little while previously would have been, "That sort of thing is not my style, Lord". However, I was discovering that if we are open to be led by the Holy Spirit, He is very good at readily adapting our style to whatever situation we happen to be in.

I had been talking about the coffee-pot, and how through the power of the cross, Jesus could remove the lid, taking from us our fears and guilt. I sensed that the Lord wanted to relieve many people of their burdens that night. When we prayed together, there was a great feeling of "release";

never have I heard people sing the words of Wesley's hymn with so much heart:

> My chains fell off, my heart was free,
> I rose, went forth and followed Thee.

Many people were "converted" that night, and nearly forty came forward for prayer to be baptised in the Holy Spirit, among them the local Roman Catholic priest!

On the third and last evening of the conference I spoke about the empowering of the Holy Spirit to enable us to witness and love in the name of Jesus. It seemed from the air of expectancy and from the way the Spirit led, that there would be far too many people wanting prayer, for me to pray individually with everyone.

I invited all who wanted the Holy Spirit to anoint them with power, to stand. About two hundred and fifty people must have stood as I asked the Lord to pour His Spirit upon us. It was one of those occasions when you could almost hear Him descend. What was certainly audible was the result of His coming, for people began to praise the Lord in tongues and soon there were hundreds of people singing in the Spirit. Many of them would never have known that such a thing was possible before that evening.

At the end of that meeting I couldn't help reflecting how remarkable it was that only a few years before I had been such a shy, timid individual. Now I could stand up without fear and speak to hundreds of people with power and authority. Later in my bedroom I fell on my face before the Lord — for all the power, the authority and the glory are His. I knew that without Him I would be useless.

My experience at Southport had opened up new dimensions of ministry. The tradition in which I had been brought up had taught me to frown upon so called "conversion experiences". They were usually dismissed as being emotional imaginings. Conversion, I was taught, should be regarded as a life-long, gradual process.

There is truth in this. Because we have received Jesus into

our lives as Lord and Saviour, that does not mean that every part of us is yet converted to Him. He will continue to lay claim to more areas of our lives that are not yet under His Lordship.

However, I had to acknowledge now, that for many people a life lived with Jesus began with a very definite experience of conversion. For some this was followed immediately by baptism in the Holy Spirit; for others, there was a delay of weeks, months, sometimes many years, before they knew the release of the power of the Spirit in their lives.

After the Southport conference the Lord said to me: "You realise that what I have done here, I can do at St. Hugh's."

"Yes Lord, I know you can!" was my reply. So it did not surprise me that He began to speak to us about having guest services at St. Hugh's.

Our new service of Evening Praise had continued to develop. Our attitude to worship had changed completely over a period of time. We no longer thought of doing our Christian duty by "going to a service"; instead we expected to meet the Lord in our worship, to know the reality of His presence amongst us. We expected to give ourselves to the Lord in adoration and praise; waiting upon Him in silence, or at the other extreme, lifting our voices to Him as we sang in the Spirit together. The point of our worship was that the Father be glorified and Jesus magnified in our hearts; we therefore needed the Holy Spirit to lead us, to anoint all who spoke and to fill everyone with praise and joy. We expected Him to reveal Himself more deeply to us through His Word on every occasion; and during the service we expected Him to be doing things in us, to further change us into His likeness. As we allowed ourselves to be open to the manifestation of the prayer gifts then God could speak directly to His children.

We expected a great deal — and the Lord always supplied more than we expected! It didn't matter if the service lasted for two or even three hours. Who would want to rush home when we were experiencing God's presence in such a real way? Even when the service had formally ended many people would stay to pray with one another, or to have fellowship in the Spirit together.

We had found that many people coming into our normal services had been touched deeply by the Lord's presence. This had often led them to "Know Jesus" groups and so to a real experience of Him in their lives. The idea of a guest service was to invite as many non-Christian friends as possible and present them with the Gospel.

The Church was packed for the first of these and many people's lives began to change that night. The opportunity was given for them to make a decision for Christ; and an invitation was given to join a new "Know Jesus" group which was to begin the following week.

At the end of the service the church was scattered with groups of people counselling and praying with the newcomers. We were truly beginning to minister as a body.

Guest services became a regular feature of our life together. They were important to the members of St. Hugh's, as well as the guests, for they were opportunities for us to renew our commitment to the Lord.

We became conscious of the importance of not looking back to an experience of the Holy Spirit that had once empowered our lives. Rather, we needed to be under His continual anointing, to be experiencing the release of more of the life of Jesus within us. The more our lives were open to Him, the more He was going to possess every part of us.

9 Asking and Receiving

"If I HAD my car here," a priest said angrily, "I would pack my bags and leave this evening!"

I was speaking at a healing conference in Cardiff, and felt that I should talk about healing within the context of the complete ministry of the Holy Spirit in our lives. The reaction to this was interesting! Most of the people attending that conference had come to hear about healing — not to be challenged deeply about their own spiritual lives and asked to face up to the inadequacies of their ministries!

That evening the situation was somewhat volatile. By the end of the conference nearly everyone had been baptised in the Holy Spirit. That same priest wrote to me some weeks later to tell me about the effects of those few days on his life.

The first and most dramatic effect was the return to normal size of my ankle. I went to see the doctor on the day we finished, for treatment, and he wanted to know what had happened, because this condition was of long standing. I have not used a walking stick since. My baby daughter's rare disease of the blood capillaries had "mysteriously" cleared up to everyone's astonishment, even the doctors from Great Ormond Street. How about that, eh?

He went on to talk of his new joy-filled life in the Spirit. We had invited the sisters who looked after the Retreat

House, to come to any of the conference sessions when they were free to do so. One of the sisters came from Sweden and had been in the community for five years. She was very unhappy and was due to leave within a few weeks. She had been trying to find the Lord through a life of discipline and obedience, and had failed. For years she had prayed that the Lord would make Himself real to her.

"I sensed there was something different about this conference," she told me. "I gave the Lord one last chance and decided to come into your talk." It so happened that it was the one about the baptism in the Holy Spirit.

This sister recognised the need for healing in her life, and longed to have a personal knowledge of God. "But these things always seemed beyond my reach," she said. "Nobody gave me any hope of ever finding the Lord or receiving the healing I needed."

That evening she poured out her heart. The Lord was releasing all the bitterness and disappointment of the past years. I couldn't help thinking, as I listened to her, what a tortured sort of existence it must have been for her — going through all the outward forms of prayer, without knowing the reality of Christ deep within her. I have since learned that this is a problem shared by many other sisters living in community. When she had finished, I suggested that we should pray. We asked the Lord to forgive her, to heal her and to fill her.

Never have I seen such a transformation in a person, but by now I was growing accustomed to the way in which the Lord could change people's lives. When I spoke to this sister the following morning, I was talking to an entirely different person. She was radiant.

It was a great joy to meet her again, over a year later, at an international conference. When she left the community, she had returned to Sweden and had been used to bring others to experience the release of the Spirit in their lives.

I have learned how important it is to bring people into a relationship with the Lord, before praying with them to be healed. There are occasions when this is not possible, for practical reasons; and at other times the Lord moves in a sovereign way, bringing healing into a person's life, in order to assure him of His love.

Jesus is concerned with each individual as a whole person. He is not concerned with only one part of the body or a part of a mind that is filled with anxiety. He wants to bring healing and wholeness of body, mind and spirit into the lives of God's children. Certainly one must resist the temptation to thoughtlessly pray and lay hands on people, simply hoping that something will happen as a result.

One Saturday I received a telephone call from someone belonging to another church on the other side of Luton. "I have a friend from Scotland staying with me for the weekend. She is in desperate need of healing. Could you possibly see her please?"

We arranged a meeting that afternoon. The lady from Scotland was in her thirties and was almost completely deaf.

"I had meningitis when I was four years old," she told me. "My hearing has grown worse ever since, and now I can hardly hear at all. I am doing a welfare job that I love: but I shall have to resign soon if I cannot hear."

Time was not on her side — nor was it on mine. I had an extremely heavy schedule that weekend. The temptation to pray and "hope for the best" was great. Fortunately I listened to the Spirit!

"The Lord is interested in you," I said, "not just your ears."

There wasn't time for me to ask her to talk about herself, but for the next half hour I spoke to her about the Holy Spirit and how she needed to bring to the Lord all her fears, guilt and doubt.

We agreed to meet together for prayer before the evening service on the following day, before she had to begin her journey back to Scotland.

When she prayed she poured out to the Lord a life that seemed in a complete and hopeless muddle, and was certainly opposed to the purpose of God.

"Well, Lord, you are a gracious God;" I prayed silently,

"we are going to need to see your graciousness here."

We asked the Lord to forgive her, to heal the misery in her life and fill her with the Holy Spirit. She was immediately liberated and began praising and thanking Him. It was obvious she was going to take a new life back with her to Scotland.

It was almost as an afterthought that I placed my hands over her ears: "Lord, please restore the hearing of your child."

Until then, I had needed to shout to make her hear me when speaking to her or praying with her.

"Can you hear, now?" I asked quietly.

She turned and looked at me, her face radiant. "Did you shout then?" she asked.

"No," I replied.

"Speak to me, speak to me," she said.

I went on talking quietly, until my voice was drowned by her saying: "I can hear, I can hear. Oh, thank you Lord, thank you."

She almost ran out of church into the arms of her friend.

It is wonderful to be healed by the Lord; even greater to be healed and given a new life in the Spirit. Often when someone needs healing, He will use the opportunity to introduce that person to a new dimension of Christian experience.

Penny, a young Christian school teacher, had a serious physical condition; her body could not cope with the fat content in food. She was eating very little and was literally wasting away. All the medical treatment she had received proved fruitless, and she had so little energy that it was becoming impossible for her to teach. God was her only hope.

Her headmaster asked if he could bring her to see me. I readily agreed and later discovered that not only the staff, but the entire school was asking the Lord to bless that meeting.

I talked to Penny about baptism in the Holy Spirit and she went away to prepare to offer herself to the Lord. When we prayed a week later (again well supported by the whole junior school) Penny was filled with the Holy Spirit. We asked the Lord to heal her. Of course, in a case like this you cannot see visibly what God is doing but Penny knew within herself that He was healing her.

Some weeks later she wrote to me:

It is with great joy that I write this letter to you to tell you of the wonderful workings of the Holy Spirit in my life. The Lord is continuing to heal me and each day I feel that much stronger. It was truly wonderful how He so filled me with His Holy Spirit and gave me the strength to go back to school for a full day without any need for a rest — but that was not all!

The Lord's healing is indeed complete and I am finding that I am gradually being able to tolerate more and more fat, which is truly wonderful, and I am now able to eat school meals again without having to watch every mouthful! I have felt more and more the desire to praise God in every moment of my life and I know that He has, in His mercy and love, used even me to His glory.

Being members of The Body of Christ we should not need to depend solely on our own prayer. It is a great advantage to be surrounded by others who are praying with faith.

Helen, a radiographer, had damaged her back lifting her patients and was told by her doctor to rest. Believing in the power of the Lord, she asked Jesus to heal her. He did, in many ways, although her back did not seem to be much better.

Her father had been ill with cancer for some years and surgery had been necessary on more than one occasion. While she was still resting her back, Helen received news that he was about to enter hospital for another operation. Because of the seriousness of the situation, his surgeon agreed to delay this for a week, so that he could visit his daughter.

"I want to bring Daddy to the prayer meeting tonight,"

Helen said to me. "I know the Lord will heal him." Helen's faith was high; her father was not so confident. He was a Christian and had been praying for years, but it seemed to him that the Lord didn't want to heal him.

Helen too wanted to receive the laying on of hands that night.

The vicarage lounge was crowded as usual and there was a great sense of praise in the room. I laid hands on Helen, and then moved to her father's side. She joined me and we both laid hands on him together. As we prayed, everybody in the room burst spontaneously into song. "To God be the glory, great things He has done." There was no visible evidence that the Lord had done anything but Jesus said, "Whatever you ask in prayer believe that you receive it, and you will." (Mark 11: 24)

A few days later he entered hospital and was prepared for surgery. During the pre-operative examination it was discovered that all the cancer tumours had completely disappeared. Helen's father was discharged, without needing an operation.

Helen's faith was answered that night, much to everyone's delight. That was a year ago; yet Helen herself is still not completely healed. Why her father's healing should have been so immediate and her own so gradual, only the Lord knows. His wisdom is greater than ours, and we have to work according to His timetable, not ours!

Sometimes people need to be brought to a point of faith before their healing can be complete. Time and time again, we have seen that God does not expect us to "go it alone" when we have any need. As members of His Body, we should be prepared to share that need with our brothers and sisters in Christ. "The gifts of healing" that St. Paul refers to are gifts for the Body of Christ.

Graham was suffering from a hiatus hernia which had perforated his diaphragm; he was in considerable discomfort, and it seemed that surgery would be necessary. Although a prayer and healing group met at his house, he had not asked for healing.

His wife, Mary, grew very concerned about this. She had been healed sometime before, when her neck, stiff with arthritis, had been released by the Lord as we prayed. Finally, she asked me to go and see Graham. I agreed, although I would have preferred the request to have come from him.

He was obviously embarrassed when I said; "Why haven't you asked for healing?"

"Well, everybody around here who prays for healing seems to be healed," Graham replied. "Suppose I ask the Lord to heal me and He doesn't — where does that place me?"

This was a very natural fear. It is easier to believe that God will heal others; much harder to believe that He will heal you.

I assured Graham that people were only being healed because of God's love for them. What right did he have to think that God loved everybody at St. Hugh's, except him? There was certainly no justification for believing such a thing; to do so, would be to deny God's love. Graham agreed that we should pray together. I knew he was still full of doubts, but the Lord was capable of dealing with them!

After a few days of preparation, we met to pray, just before Graham's next hospital visit. The pain began to ease, but he knew that he was not completely healed. A decision was to be made by the surgeon as to whether to operate or not. So Graham went to the hospital with some apprehension.

Imagine his surprise when he was told; "We're sorry, we seem to have lost all your X-rays. We will have to take another set."

A few weeks breathing space. The Lord had begun to heal Graham — and he knew it. We arranged to pray again and this time he could pray with more faith. He no longer doubted the Father's will to heal him.

The pain went. And when Graham returned to the hospital, he was discharged.

Jesus said, "As you have believed, so let it be" (Matt. 9:29 NEB). There have been a number of other occasions when I have known the Lord to build up faith in similar ways. He does not want to heal only our bodily functions; He also wants to increase our faith in the living God.

On the other hand, there are times when the Lord moves us to pray with people in the most unlikely situations, when there appears to be little or no faith in God. Tony had not been filled with the Spirit for long, when his father became very ill. He had gall stones, and would need surgery. However, he also had a very weak heart and the doctors were afraid that an operation might prove fatal. Tony asked me to go and see his father. I sat by the side of his bed, and for an hour could hardly get a word in edgeways as I listened to a continuous list of reasons why a person doesn't need to believe in God or go to church. You could hardly imagine a less likely situation for healing to take place, and I knew Tony was praying for his father to be healed.

When he had finished speaking, I felt moved to say quite simply, "Jesus loves you, and He wants to heal you."

"I can't believe that!" was the curt reply.

I talked about two healing miracles that had happened recently; he listened without comment.

"I can see that you don't believe that Jesus can heal you," I concluded, "but do you believe that I believe He can?"

"Oh, I can see that you believe in this healing," he replied.

"Well, do you mind if I pray with you before I go?" I asked.

"You can, if you want to," he said.

I laid hands on his head, and asked Jesus to pour His healing life into him.

As I entered the hospital ward three days later, a group of doctors was leaving his bedside, looking very perplexed.

When he saw me coming, Tony's father shouted across the ward: "I'm a fraud! Here I am, taking up a hospital bed, and they won't let me go home, because they can't find anything wrong with me!"

The doctors could not understand how the yellow jaundice (which often accompanies this complaint) could disappear so rapidly. Nor could they discover what had happened to the stones, which had not passed out of the body. The only scare in the next few days was when they contemplated doing an exploratory operation to hunt for them! Fortunately, they decided against this course, and discharged him, without his needing the surgeon's knife.

That healing was an act of sheer love and grace on the Lord's part. No one can ever deserve to be healed.

I received a message from the hospital that a little girl of about two had been involved in a fire and was critically ill. When I arrived at her bedside, she was not expected to live for more than an hour or two. When I looked at her, I could see why. Never had I seen a human body in such a mess. Parts of her arms and legs were charred in a hideous way. She seemed to be in a semi-conscious daze, but I was assured by the medical staff that she was in no pain.

"Lord, what a mess!" I thought, "But you are the Lord of miracles. Nothing is impossible for you. I believe you can heal even this little one."

I prayed with the girl. As I laid hands over her (obviously she could not be touched) her body seemed to respond.

When I left the hospital it was lunchtime; I didn't feel like eating. Instead, I went into the church, flung myself down and cried in the Spirit. I suppose I was sharing the grief of the Lord. Never before had I prayed for so long in tongues. It was as if I was beseeching Him, imploring Him for the life of that child.

That evening we had a combined meeting of our prayer groups, so everyone joined in the prayer battle.

The following day, she was still alive, much to the amazement of the hospital staff. Again, I was assured that she was in no pain.

The prayer continued day after day. The little girl was still alive, but there still didn't appear to be very much improvement in her physical condition. One week after the accident, during my morning time of prayer, the Lord said to me: "Release her."

"Very well, Lord, if that is your will; I release her into your loving care."

The little girl died peacefully.

God taught us a great deal about faith and the power of prayer through that incident. He also underlined for me the need to hear and obey what He was saying.

I did not find this lesson easy to learn, particularly when I needed healing myself.

Life was becoming quite hectic, it was a job keeping up with all that the Holy Spirit was doing amongst us at St. Hugh's. Because we were all "new" in the Spirit, we had no ready-made counsellors, people with many years experience of life in the Spirit, who could be of help to those just entering into this new dimension.

This meant that I was carrying a considerable load personally. I was wearing myself out and began to have the warning signs of trouble. I suddenly began to suffer with what can only be described as chronic indigestion. It was with me all day long and although it did not prevent me from working, it was a continual nuisance.

The most natural thing was to ask God to heal me. When I prayed, the Lord answered: "No wonder your body is suffering, the way you are treating it." The message was clear: "Ease up!"

"How can I, Lord?" I answered. It was all very well for Him to tell me to ease up; the chance to do so would have been gratefully accepted. It is never wise to argue with God, although we do it more than we would care to admit!

While at Cardiff I asked people to pray with me. Still I was not healed, but was given assurance by the Lord that my healing was in His hands.

For a while I tried to catch a few minutes' rest during the day, but the good intention did not last for long. I was soon working at the old pace and the indigestion became worse. It was sometimes accompanied by spasms of pain in the chest that I would dismiss with a nonchalant "it's nothing" if Caroline happened to catch me wincing.

The tempter had a field day at times. "Why don't you go

to the doctor? A few pills and you will feel as right as rain!" There were times when I considered this possibility. Yet on every occasion I was filled with peace that my healing would come from Jesus.

Satan attacked again: "The trouble with you is that you are proud! The great believer in healing can't admit defeat and go to the doctor!" The source of these accusations was easy to discern.

The Lord used these months to good effect. When you are not healed of something immediately you begin to search your soul to discover if there is anything in your life that could prevent the power of Christ being received. Several areas of my life needed the attention of the Holy Spirit and He led me to a deeper commitment to God. But still no physical healing.

Instead of being able to ease up the amount of work became more and more impossible. But I could not believe that the Lord would allow me to suffer physically for doing His work. He had been teaching us as a church family to share our needs; but I didn't want to make a fuss about a bit of indigestion. There were many more important things to be concerned with than that!

After five months the Lord prevailed. During one of our Friday evening prayer and praise sessions in the vicarage, He said to me: "Ask for healing!" I knew what that would involve.

"I have a confession to make," I started. "I have not really been fit for the past five months." That was not news. I was fed up with people saying, "Colin, you look so tired!" I explained how the Lord had told me what to do, and I had refused to listen.

"I want you to pray with me, please. I would like someone to lay hands on me and ask that I be healed, and given the grace to heed what the Lord is saying."

When I had asked the Lord's forgiveness, Terry stood up, stepped over a few people, laid his hands on my head and said: "Please Jesus, heal my brother Colin". Terry, you will remember, had once been a "skin-head"!

Again that sense of inner peace, the conviction that Jesus was healing me, but still the discomfort was there. I began to thank God for His healing; I knew He was going to honour the prayer of my brothers and sisters.

He did. For the next three days I slept and slept and slept. I could hardly keep my eyes open. I would stagger out of bed for morning worship and prayer, do whatever was vitally necessary — and fall asleep again. It was as if someone had given me a heavy sleeping draught.

After the three days I felt refreshed. And there was no pain, no indigestion, no discomfort. "Thank you Jesus. You certainly taught me a lesson!"

You can't beat the Lord: so you may as well go along with what He says.

10   Fire!

I COULD HEAR a trumpet playing.

We were singing Wesley's rousing hymn: "O for a thousand tongues to sing, my dear Redeemer's praise" — a favourite at St. Hugh's.

When announcing the hymn, I had said: "There may not be a thousand of us here tonight, but we are joining with the whole host of heaven in praising God. Let us ask the Lord to make us aware that we are part of that great worshipping company as we sing."

It was during the second verse that I heard the trumpet. I didn't take much notice at first, as John, a member of the church family, would often accompany the organ on his trumpet. I looked towards the back of the church expecting to see him. He wasn't there!

I listened more intently and realised that I could hear not one trumpet, but several, blending beautifully with the organ. I was so certain that this was not my imagination that, when the hymn ended, I said to everyone: "I heard trumpets during that hymn." Several people nodded and after the service confirmed that they too had heard the heavenly trumpets.

Later Stewart, our organist, said to me: "Something strange happened to the organ; the trumpet stop refused to work during that hymn. It was working perfectly up until then; it worked perfectly afterwards, but it would not work at all during that hymn."

Things like that don't really happen — do they?

Many people are only prepared to believe what they can accept rationally. Our God is not One who can be limited by our tiny minds. A miracle does not have to be an enormous event, like the feeding of the five thousand. It can be something much more personal; for example, the occasion when Simon Peter caught a fish with a coin in it, to pay the tax for Jesus and himself.

Miracles are signs of God's sovereign power and His love for us. If His children have a need, why shouldn't the Creator of Heaven and earth perform a miracle to meet that need?

Of course there will be those who will want to explain all these things away. For nearly two thousand years there have been those who have said that Jesus was walking on a sandbank, not the sea; or that the boy offering his loaves and fish to Him encouraged everybody else to produce their own sandwiches! Miracles are the easiest things to explain away if you don't want to believe them. Don't expect to see many in your own life if you do!

Miracles have become a natural part of the lives of many members of our church family, because the Lord has given us the faith to believe that they will happen. St. Paul includes miracles among the gifts of the Holy Spirit. Wherever God is moving with power in the lives of His children, we can expect such things to be taking place. A group of us from St. Hugh's were waiting in Trafalgar Square for the Festival of Light rally to begin. I was sitting on a wall watching the crowds gathering, when I became aware of a woman making her way resolutely towards us from the other side of the square.

She came straight up to me and said: "Are you from Luton?"

"Yes."

"Do you know Colin Urquhart?"

"I am Colin Urquhart," I replied.

It was her turn to be surprised.

"There is a young man in our group who has just moved to Luton and wants to worship at your church. His name is also Colin."

I told the woman that we would be delighted to welcome him, made a note of his address and said that a member of our congregation would call for him the following morning, to bring him to Parish Communion.

It was perplexing to know how, out of all the thousands of people in Trafalgar Square, the woman should have chosen to come up to me. I put it down to extraordinary guidance by the Holy Spirit.

Many months later I discussed this event with Colin and remarked on how amazing it had seemed.

"Well, she saw the banner you were carrying," said Colin.

"What banner?" I asked.

"The banner with 'Luton' written on it."

I was not carrying a banner, nor were any of the others in our party!

God is Lord of the elements. Several of us have had experiences involving the weather. One evening a group of people were going by car to an evening meeting at Bedford. There was thick fog. It became so dense that the only sensible thing to do was to turn back. They stopped and prayed. When they opened their eyes the fog had completely disappeared. They arrived at the meeting on time, praising the Lord!

There was another occasion when I was going to a meeting in thick fog. I had to find a vicarage in the middle of a housing estate that I did not know. I was competely lost and prayed, "Please Lord, lead me there."

"Turn around." I turned the car round. "Straight down this road." I obeyed. "Left here . . . right here . . . round the roundabout . . . turn left here." And there I was, right outside the house. "Thank you, Lord."

Then there was the time when I had to go to Sheffield for a meeting of the Archbishops' Council on Evangelism. I was returning to Luton on the M1 Motorway, listening to a cassette tape-recording I had made, containing some of the promises of God from the Bible. I was travelling at seventy miles an hour, when I suddenly realised that all the other traffic was moving at a much slower pace. Not without reason, either. An extremely strong wind was making driving hazardous.

However, my car, which is not normally very good at road-holding in high winds, seemed to be unaffected. Nobody else was attempting to drive at more than fifty. There seemed little point in slowing down — until the tape ran out. I was immediately buffeted by the wind and was forced to lessen my speed. With one hand, I reversed the cassette. The Word of God poured out again and I could drive at seventy miles an hour. What is this power in the Word? I do not fully understand, but I would not deliberately put the Lord to the test!

If the Lord can heal human bodies He can heal anything, even motor cars. There have been several "impossible" events involving cars.

A group of us were driving to the south coast for a few days of ministry. We had reached the outskirts of Watford when the car suddenly started to make the most appalling clanging noise. I know very little about cars, but it seemed a very serious and expensive noise. Unfortunately we were passing some road works when the car ground to a halt. There we were, stuck in the middle of the road.

What would reasonably intelligent, sensible people do? Get out and push of course! We prayed.

Then we drove to Bournemouth, praising the Lord.

On another occasion my own car started making a most strange noise half a mile from home. By driving very slowly, I just made it to the house. I telephoned the garage which was two or three miles away and arranged for it to be repaired.

'I'll ask Tony to tow me there," I said to Caroline, "the car will never make it." But Tony had gone to work early.

"I'll try to drive it there and hope for the best." I started reversing down the drive. The noise was awful. I had only gone a few feet when I stopped. "No good," I said to Caroline. "I suppose I shall have to ask the garage to come and tow it in."

"Why don't you pray?" Caroline said.

"That's the kind of ridiculous suggestion I like," I replied.

After praying, I climbed into the car again and began reversing. The noise was enough to waken anyone in the neighbourhood who had decided to have a late morning in bed. "Trust me," the Lord said. I drove off down the road at about five miles an hour. The noise stopped. Slowly I increased speed. Still no noise.

Try as he would, the garage mechanic could find nothing wrong.

By the way, the Lord hasn't a grudge against garages. My car is regularly serviced and properly maintained; but it is good to know the Lord is willing to help, whenever needed.

These signs of the Father's love for His children arise out of a life lived by faith in Him. This is true of the healing that we have known over the past three years.

Sometimes people say, "I wish I had more faith!" Jesus said that we only need a little faith, the size of a mustard seed, and we will be able to move mountains. The Lord was referring to His faith, which He is wanting to give to us. We can endeavour to have buckets full of our own faith and see nothing happen as a result.

"Ask and it will be given you", (Matt. 7:7) Jesus said. Often we dare not ask, because we do not believe that we shall receive. We need that gift of faith that comes from the Holy Spirit, to encourage us to ask when the situation looks completely hopeless. That principle applies to healing, to our problems or to any situation where we have a need.

If we are asking with faith, then we can praise the Lord in every difficulty. The power of God seems to be released whenever we begin to praise Him in the middle of such circumstances. Another spiritual gift that comes in very useful on these occasions, is "tongues"!

There was a time when three people in our church had serious problems that had gone on for weeks. "This is ridiculous," I thought. "I am sure the Lord doesn't want things to continue like this." I went into church and began to pray in tongues about each of these three situations. Within days, two of the problems were completely solved and the third had changed dramatically. The Holy Spirit knows what to pray, better than we do with our limited understanding.

In May 1973, someone tried to set fire to St. Hugh's church building. Between eleven and twelve o'clock at night, this person (or persons) lit three fires: one on the altar, one on a table, and the other among a pile of books near the entrance.

At 6.45 the following morning I went into church to prepare for Holy Communion and was met by a thick wall of smoke. As I opened the door, the smoke rushed out causing me to stagger back.

I could see flames just inside the door, so I ran into the church hall for water and managed to put that fire out. I could hear crackling noises coming from the direction of the altar at the other end of the building. The smoke was so dense that I could only take a few steps before being driven back. I rang for the fire brigade.

The first person to appear on the scene was police sergeant Mick. The fire brigade soon arrived and in a few minutes had dealt with the matter efficiently. Meanwhile, people began to arrive for the Communion service. "Someone must have it in for your church," sergeant Mick said. Nobody answered. We were all too busy praising the Lord that the whole place hadn't burnt down.

Later the fire chief stood in the church and shook his head in disbelief. He had examined the charred wood at one corner of the altar and declared that the fire had definitely been burning all night.

"I cannot understand," he said, "why the whole place

didn't go up in flames. A building with this volume of air should have burned easily."

I don't think he would have accepted our explanation!

Very little damage was done. We needed a new top to the altar, some scout flags had been destroyed and the insurance company agreed to redecorate the whole church, because of the smell left by the smoke.

And sergeant Mick? Well, he might not have had many answers given him that morning, but this group of people singing, rejoicing and praising the Lord just after their church had been set on fire, was out of his usual run of duty!

Some weeks later he was radiant and rejoicing himself. He had been baptised in the Holy Spirit.

A few days after the fire, our Bishop arrived at the vicarage late one evening. He had heard about the fire and had come to express his concern. I told him what had happened to which he replied, "I thought that if any church could cope with fire, it would be St. Hugh's!"

I am often asked how our Bishop views what is happening at our church. Some seem to find it difficult to understand how we can be part of the established church, and yet remain free in the Spirit.

All over the world God is renewing His church in power and in love. Who can take exception if St. Hugh's is beginning to manifest something of this power and love? Certainly our Bishop would not want to. I have the opportunity from time to time to keep him informed of the way our corporate life is developing here, under the direction of the Holy Spirit. He has shown understanding and increasing sympathy for the work that God is doing among us, and has expressed his confidence in us as a church, and in me as his representative in this parish.

11 A Single Loaf

"LORD, SHOW US how you want us to go out and witness!"
Many people at St. Hugh's were being moved to pray with
greater intensity for all who did not know Jesus, especially
those living in our district. We were very conscious of the
thousands of people on our housing estate, untouched by
the Gospel.

We knew that it was no good having any man-inspired
evangelistic activities, because they would prove fruitless.
We were prepared for Him to say just about anything,
except what He did say:

"YOU ARE TO LOVE ONE ANOTHER THAT THE
WORLD MIGHT BELIEVE."

For the first time since the Spirit began to fill our lives, we
had trouble on our hands.

Week after week, we could not get away from the theme
of love — in worship, in preaching, in prayer and in prophecy. Nobody minded that at first, because we knew that
God had put a new love into our hearts, a love for Him and a
love for one another.

"YOU ARE TO LOVE ONE ANOTHER THAT THE
WORLD MIGHT BELIEVE." Immediately, there were two
groups of people in the church family. There were those who
said: "We *do* love one another. The Lord has given us a
tremendous affection for each other. Why, even people from
outside our church comment on the wonderful love there is
here."

The other group said: "The Lord is right! He has given us a love for one another. We feel this, but we haven't yet faced up to to the real issue of putting it into action."

Jesus said, "Greater love has no man than this, that a man lay down his life for his friends" (John 15:13). I had never thought very deeply about that verse, which seemed to be a reference made by Jesus to His imminent crucifixion. Certainly, I had never connected it with the preceding verse: "This is my commandment, that you love one another *as I have loved you*" (John 15:12).

For Jesus, love meant laying down His life for His friends. We are to love in the same way that Jesus loved us. That means we need to lay down our lives for our friends. We hadn't begun to do that — yet! Nor was it easy to understand what it meant in practical terms. It did not seem that the church at large had faced up to this command given by Jesus. As I thought and prayed about this, the Lord began to show me that we at St. Hugh's needed to be a community. I did not understand how this could be possible, because my mind was conditioned by traditional concepts of community. We were beginning to share our lives more deeply, but how could we live a common life, without living under the same roof? How could a bunch of ordinary families, in a housing estate parish, become a community?

The Lord supplied the answer in an unexpected way.

A Roman Catholic ecumenical society arranged a conference entitled "The Holy Spirit in the Churches today". I was there under protest! Right up to the last minute I would have been glad of an excuse not to go because of the pressure of work at St. Hugh's. However, I felt that the Lord wanted me there, so I went.

On the first evening I prayed, "Lord what on earth am I doing here?" The following morning Kevin and Dorothy Ranaghan talked about the concept of Community, and all the way through the Lord was speaking directly to me. They told of how a group of people were beginning to commit their lives to one another, while still living in their own homes. I recognised that much of the detail of what the

Ranaghans were saying bore little relevance for our situation; but the Lord was showing me that it was possible to share a common life, while still living in separate homes.

I knew He was wanting us at St. Hugh's to commit our lives to one another in love, and was opening my eyes to see what that meant.

Fortunately, I went on holiday soon after that conference, and therefore had time to digest what the Lord was saying. We were to "love one another that the world might believe" and this meant laying down our lives for our friends. This would involve sharing our lives at every possible level — spiritually, practically and financially. I needed a holiday!

Caroline and I took the children to a beautiful place in mid-Wales. We parked our touring caravan on a farm site situated in its own little valley and close to the sea; ideal for scenery and for the children to play on the beach.

It was a good holiday, although there was a great deal going on inside me. Caroline was still not "with it" as far as the Holy Spirit was concerned. I found it impossible to get through to her and it became obvious that talking only made matters worse. This was very frustrating. When the Lord performed miracles in people's lives, it was good to be able to tell someone about them, especially my wife! I wondered what her reaction would be if I told her that I felt the Lord was leading us to lay down everything for our friends!

In the caravan there was very little time to be alone with the Lord, especially as we did not pray together. After about ten days I was missing fellowship with the Lord so desperately that I announced late one night: "I'm going out for a walk. Don't wait up for me, I may be some time."

Caroline gave me a side-ways glance: she was used to the strange ways of her husband.

It was a very dark night; no moon was visible. I reached for the camping lamp: the battery was flat! We had a replacement but try as I could, I found it impossible to unscrew the bottom of the lamp to take out the old one.

"Oh well, if the Lord wants me to see," I said to Caroline, "He'll put new life into this battery."

I closed the caravan door and began to walk along the car track through the farm site. When Jesus wanted to be alone with His Father, He went into the hills. A few days earlier I had climbed up a small one with the children, so I knew roughly the way I needed to go. Roughly was the right word. It was pitch black, the lamp still refused to work, and I stumbled and slipped on the dewy grass. When I finally reached the point I was aiming at all sense of prayer had left me! I was conscious of bleating sheep all around, and they didn't seem very impressed at the presence of a son of God in their midst!

I couldn't help thinking that I was in the wrong place!

I slithered my way down the hill, having to be very careful not to give voice to ejaculations that belonged to the old life. Eventually, I arrived back at the caravan. It was in darkness; Caroline had gone to bed.

"I may as well have some prayer here before I go in," I thought.

I took a camping chair out of the boot of the car and sat down. Immediately I was at peace. This was the right place; there was no need to go stumbling up dark hills to be with the Lord.

As I sat alongside the caravan, facing a large clump of trees, I spent several minutes resting in the Lord's love. Then I opened my eyes.

"I must be dreaming," I thought. "No, I'm awake. I must be seeing things. No, there is nothing wrong with my eyes."

The clump of trees in front of me was floodlit — that's the only way I can describe it. It is not a very good description because the light seemed to be coming from among the trees, and around the trees. Most strange. I looked and looked, but could see no source for the light. The trees were simply aglow.

Then God began to speak to me. He told me that I was about to enter a difficult time in my ministry. I was not to fear, nor was I to be discouraged from the course that He would lay before us at St. Hugh's. If I remained faithful

during the difficult time ahead, the Lord promised to lead
me into a time of greater joy. It was a great comfort when
He told me not to be concerned about Caroline; she would
come to accept His love in time.

I must have sat there for a long time, unable to speak. I
just gazed at those trees bathed in the light, "lost in wonder,
love and praise." Then eventually the light slowly faded and
the trees were just a very dark and heavy shadow. I went to
bed. Caroline was asleep.

When we returned to Luton, I knew that we had to get
down to this business of loving one another. We had been
talking about it for months, now we had to do it.

When the Holy Spirit began to renew our church, Peter,
Eunice and their children, Paul and Lorraine, were the first
newcomers to arrive. Peter had become disillusioned with
the world's way of living and was seeking some real meaning
and purpose in life.

"I came to St. Hugh's as a last resort," he told me later. "I
had lived just down the road from the church for years, but
had never set foot inside the place. Immediately I did so, I
knew there was something different here, and I was struck
by the conviction and authority of the preaching."

Both Peter and Eunice were baptised in the Holy Spirit a
few months later. He and others became aware that he was
to give up his employment and work full-time for God in the
parish. To do this, he would have to be dependant upon the
church family for financial support.

It seemed that the Lord was saying: "You are to love one
another, and I am giving you Peter and Eunice to see
whether you are prepared to do it!"

I told our two churchwardens that I believed the Lord
wanted to make St. Hugh's a community of love and praise,
and that Peter was being led to work full-time for the Lord.
They were unimpressed on both counts! I remembered the
Lord's warning to me that the way was going to be difficult
and that I must persevere.

"I am going to say all this to the church family at Parish

Communion on Sunday," I said. "We will have a special time of prayer next Friday. If this is what the Lord wants He will confirm it."

"Lord," I prayed on the Saturday night, "I want to be absolutely sure that this is the right time and the right way for me to present this to everyone."

The words "Hosea, chapter fourteen" came into my mind. Underlined in my *New English Bible* was a phrase from verse eight: "I have spoken and I affirm it." That settled it!

The sermon created quite a stir. We were about to tread on new ground. Some welcomed the prospect:

"It seems the Lord has been wanting us to go on with Him, but we haven't seen how."

"I have been longing for something like this."

"I feel the Lord really wants this."

Others reacted differently: "Now wait a minute. We have gone along with you so far, and are grateful to the Lord for the love He has shown us and the praise He has given us. But let's not go mad! I want to continue as I am at present. Praise the Lord that He has come to share my way of life!"

When it came to the Friday prayer meeting, we didn't tell the Lord what we wanted; we simply opened our hearts to Him. "What do you want, Lord?"

By the end of the evening He had given us, through a number of different people, a series of prophetic visions. I can only recount some of them.

"You are like separate snowflakes," the Lord said, "which can easily melt. I am going to roll you into a ball so that you are compacted tightly together. Do not be afraid to let me do that to you, for then you shall not melt. And as I roll you into a ball so other snowflakes shall be added to you and it will increase in size."

We were beginning to appreciate that the Lord does not intend His children to live isolated lives, like separate fragile snowflakes.

"You are like separate grains of flour," He said through

our lay reader, Nick. "I will add water and yeast to you and I will knead you into my dough. And I will put you into my oven and make you a single loaf of my baking."

Whatever was going to happen to us, the Lord was going to do it. It seemed that we were going to undergo a radical change. We were starting as grains of flour and were going to end up as a single loaf!

During succeeding months, I often thought about the process of making bread. Dough needs to be pounded!

"Do not be like pebbles on a beach," the Lord said through someone else, "for they are washed to and fro by the tides, and are piled into heaps but can never be truly united. You are like separate rivulets that can easily be stopped up. I will cause these rivulets to become a single river that shall flow with such force that it shall sweep aside all obstacles!"

The message was clear. The Lord was going to do something to change our way of life. That evening we were left with a burning question: "What does this mean in practice?"

"Let's meet again next Friday," I suggested.

During the following week I prayed that the Lord would make it clear in practical terms what He wanted. He answered that prayer at a most unlikely time.

On the Thursday evening I was about to rush off to a group meeting, when I realised that I had left a book I needed in the church. I picked up the book, and was about to hurry off when a voice within stopped me.

"Go and sit down." Recognising the voice, I obeyed. "Write this down," it continued. The words came at just the speed that enabled me to put them down on paper.

As I was in such a rush, I stuffed the paper into my pocket and it was only later that I was able to digest what the Lord had said.

You are to commit your lives to me — to be led by my Holy Spirit.

You are to promise obedience to the leading of My Spirit within the Community.

You are to worship and pray together in the Spirit.

You are to love one another — have that relationship with one another that is pleasing to me.

You are to be concerned with the spreading of my Word of Truth in this parish.

You are to show the quality of love I require of my children to Christians of other churches.

I, the Lord, promise to lead you in all things — to enrich greatly your lives with many blessings, if you will only be faithful to me in this. I will enter into an agreement with you, an agreement which I will honour because of my love for you. Let no one be afraid of entering into an agreement with me, for by doing this you will be bound closer to me in love.

I hadn't expected the Lord to speak in that way! It all seemed to be there: commitment, obedience, worship, prayer, love, evangelism, witness.

By the following evening, this was typed and duplicated, so that everybody could have a copy to study. Again, God led our prayer and showed us that we must not be afraid to share our lives together. However, many members of the church were afraid, and those who were expressing their fears most audibly were those who had not been at the prayer meetings!

I felt I was in a dilemma. I was absolutely convinced that the Lord wanted us to begin to share our lives in every possible way. I was also aware that if we tried to make this happen, we would fall flat on our spiritual faces. The Lord had caused everything to happen in the past and *He* was going to do the kneading and the baking, so that *He* could produce the new loaf.

We were concerned that nothing be done to cause a split within the family. The Lord had kept us united so far. He had taken hold of all of us together, and was leading all of us together. Whatever we decided to do was either going to cause frustration in one group of people or fear in another.

"Lord what now?".

It became apparent that He was giving us a vision of what He wanted of us, so that all the inner conflicts within the individual members of the body of Christ at St. Hugh's could be dealt with before His plan became a reality.

As the weeks passed we began to see that community did not mean any one particular thing in our situation. Living as a community was going to mean different things to different groups of people within the church.

Many of our pre-conceived ideas of what this word "community" meant would have to go. Before we could commit ourselves whole-heartedly to obey the "Six Principles" He had given us, a great deal had to be done within the lives of every one of us. We prayed a dangerous prayer: "Lord, please deal with all the unloving things about us." Immediately, these things became exposed.

We had been prepared to love other people from a distance, by doing things for them, listening to them, praying for them. We were more reticent to allow them to love us by doing things for us and giving to us. Certainly many of us did not really want to share ourselves with others.

The Lord began to deal with us and we found that deep relationships in the Spirit began to develop between small groups of people within the church family. I began to see that we already were a community and by the power of His Holy Spirit, the Lord was going to cause us to become the type of community that He wanted.

12 Living By Promise

THERE WERE SEVERAL areas of need that we had not begun to touch, including the many social problems of the housing estate. We were not equipped to deal with such problems yet. We would need a sizable group working full-time to make any real impression on the district. That would mean spiritually mature Christians who would be willing to give their lives to do this. There would also need to be people financially committed to one another, prepared to support the families of those engaged in such ministries.

If only we could jump the next few months, so that we were suddenly transformed into the sort of church that the Lord wanted! No such thing would happen; His purpose amongst us would have to be worked out. More people were being given the vision of the Lord's plan for us. To meet the situations we were faced with, we were going to require a radical change in our way of life.

Little Tony (not to be confused with the one mentioned earlier, often known as "Big" Tony) was in a terrible state when he arrived on my doorstep late one evening. He had been under psychiatric treatment for six years, and unable to work. He had taken drugs illicitly, on occasions within black magic circles.

As we talked it became apparent that Tony was bound by evil spirits. He had not been to church for years, but in his early teens had worshipped at a Brethren Assembly for some months; and so he had some knowledge of the Scriptures.

I explained to him the nature of his problem.

"I know," he replied. "I know I'm bound by evil spirits. On my way to see you I heard voices saying: 'Don't go. Don't go. Keep away from that man.' They nearly stopped me from coming."

"I'm very pleased for your sake that you ignored them, Tony," I replied, as he became more and more agitated.

"Let's pray," I suggested.

Tony asked God's forgiveness and renounced the drugs and his connections with the occult. Then I prayed and commanded the evil spirits to be bound and leave him.

Immediately, there was a change in Tony. The agitation ceased. A great peace descended on him and he began to smile.

"I'm free," he said. "Thank you, Jesus, I'm free."

Then he surprised me. "What's all this about being baptised in the Holy Spirit?" Apparently, the lady who had directed Tony to me that night had told him that people's lives were being changed through this experience.

"I want to be baptised in the Holy Spirit," he went on.

By now it was very late. "I'll need to talk to you more fully about that, Tony. Come back and see me tomorrow afternoon."

When he returned we talked together for some time. "I want to be baptised with the Holy Spirit now," Tony said. "Will you pray with me please?"

I agreed. I got up from my chair, went across the room, laid hands on Tony's head, and was just about to ask Jesus to fill him with the Holy Spirit, when he burst into prayer: "Oh Jesus, baptise me with your Spirit, please Jesus, please. Jesus, baptise me with your Holy Spirit — please."

How could the Lord refuse such a request? He filled him with the Spirit and Tony began to praise the Lord in tongues. Then he laughed and laughed and laughed. He had hardly laughed for six years; there had been little to laugh about. Caroline was on her way home in the car and passed Tony, walking along the street, still laughing. She recognised him from the previous evening.

"I've just seen that young chap walking along, laughing and singing. What on earth's happened to him?"

I hardly liked to answer. Caroline was not laughing or singing spiritually.

Little Tony's life had been changed by the Lord. He had been delivered from evil spirits and filled with the Holy Spirit. However, there was still a great deal of healing needed in his life. Above all, he would need friends who would accept and love him.

These he found at St. Hugh's and after a few weeks he was well enough to begin work. "Big" Tony, a carpenter, gave him a job as his mate. This was ideal, for it meant that "Little" Tony was with a Christian during the day and in various homes of members of the church family most evenings.

For six months he continued to improve, but then he began to show signs of restlessness. On an increasing number of evenings he would be off somewhere else; back to his old life. He denied all this at first, but there was no hiding the fact that he was trying to lead one life with the Lord and an entirely different kind of life at the same time.

Suddenly his mental condition deteriorated. We had three hectic days and nights when he stayed at the vicarage, and then he was readmitted to the psychiatric wing of the hospital. It seemed that nine months of progress had been wiped out.

I have related this incident because it highlights a problem. We offered Tony a tremendous amount of love, but it wasn't enough to cope with his situation. He needed to be living in a Christian home.

We could pray with many of the people who came to us for healing and then send them home with the Lord's blessing. There were others who needed not only prayer, but love, and a great deal of it.

To pray with some people, asking the Lord to heal them, and then to send them back to the situation that had contributed towards their problems, was going to be ineffective unless they were very strong emotionally. People like Tony were not strong, and could not cope. If the Lord was asking us to lay down our lives for our friends, then perhaps it could mean inviting those with big problems to come and live with us. However, to have someone with deep emotional problems living in your home can be a very gruelling experience. This is even more difficult if there are young children in the house, which would be the case with most members of our church family. Ideally, we wanted a large house in the country, away from the temptations of the "old life", which could be a Christian rehabilitation centre. This would require money and also the right people to run it, qualified both spiritually and medically.

The Lord was giving us the vision of what He wanted, and what we needed.

Sometimes I used to look round our congregation and say silently: "Lord, we are a very ordinary bunch of people. You seem to expect so much of us."

The reply was obvious. Had Jesus not said that much was expected of those to whom much was given? We had received a tremendous amount from the Lord, and deep down we all knew that He had not blessed us for our own spiritual self-indulgence. He was still preparing us for the real work that He wanted to do amongst us.

Even so, the Lord was showing us that our houses needed to be open and available to Him. There were many people who would benefit from living in an atmosphere of Christian love, although we were not yet equipped to deal with those who had deep emotional problems.

The Lord made it clear that if we were going to open our homes to those in need, this would have to begin at the vicarage.

"Lord," I protested, "what about Caroline?"

She had reached the point of seeking the Lord, but it was obvious that she was nowhere near ready to begin living in an extended household with others. However, I grew more and more convinced that this was what the Lord wanted; so finally I talked to Caroline about it. She has never doubted the way the Lord has led me and she reluctantly agreed that if this was what He wanted, there was no point in fighting against it.

I was filled with even greater trepidation when it seemed right that a thirty year old school teacher, separated from her husband, should move into the vicarage with her two boys and the sixteen-year-old girl who lived with them, and who was in the care of the local authority. She was a typically rebellious teenager, showing the usual signs of defiance and a contempt for the society that had made her feel unwanted and unloved.

If the vicarage was to be their home, it would mean sharing everything. It is painful to recall those first few weeks of living together.

It was not long before Caroline began to show her true feelings about the whole matter. Before they moved in, she had given the impression that she was prepared to go along with the whole thing because it was what the Lord wanted and therefore what I wanted. Once the deed was done, she began to seethe with resentment directed mainly at me. It was I who had allowed our home to become disrupted. It was I who brought another woman into the house. It was I who had wanted our lives to be invaded by strangers!

And Caroline seethed with resentment against the Lord. It was He who wanted it! It was He who allowed it! A popular song at St. Hugh's at that time began with the words: "The Lord is a great and mighty King, just and gentle with everything." As far as she was concerned, there was nothing just or gentle about God! Far from it!

Anyone who knows Caroline knows her as a quiet, lovely and lovable person. But the Caroline I was now living with suddenly seemed an entirely different person. She wanted nothing to do with me and hated the thought of me even touching her. There was hardly any communication between us. Instead of growing together in the Spirit, we were growing apart.

I felt a knife go through my heart when she said one day: "If I had anywhere to go with the children, I would walk out and leave you."

On top of all this, I had to try and make the others feel at home! Every attempt to do that made things worse with Caroline. The girl was full of rebellion at having to come and live in a vicarage; and we soon discovered that one of the boys was a very disturbed child. He suffered from serious psychological illness. The worst thing was his destructiveness, and it was almost a daily occurrence to find more of our children's toys smashed.

What a mess! How I prayed!

"Lord, what on earth is happening? What have I done to Caroline? Lord, help. Break through somehow, Lord — please."

Every time I prayed, He assured me that all would be well. On one occasion He gave me some precious words of prophecy, which I still carry around in my Bible:

Concerning your wife: Know that she is as a bright jewel in my crown. Her sincerity of heart delights me and I shall use her to point the way for many to my Kingdom. Your prayer to be united in love has been heard and I make you both this promise: As you remain faithful to me, so shall I remain faithful to you, and your love for one another shall deepen; for the Son of Righteousness shall fill your life together.

As the sun draws out the different colours of creation; so shall the Son highlight your love for one another. You have much to learn together but I will be your teacher . . ."

Although a promise from the Lord, those words seemed impossible to fulfil. However, I was learning to live by promise.

Things came to a head during the school half-term week. Usually as a family we go off in the caravan for a few days holiday. This year there were nine of us!

"I can't even have you to myself on holiday," Caroline protested. Normally she did not expect to have much time with me, except when we were away together.

I was so confused. I was sure the Lord had led this family to come and live with us. I had asked others to pray about this and they confirmed that they believed this to be God's will. But look at Caroline!

When we returned to Luton, I prayed and prayed. Every spare minute I had would be spent in the church pleading with the Lord to bring Caroline and I together — not only in human terms, but in the Spirit. "Lord, you promise to grant us our hearts' desire. This is the desire of my heart."

The following weekend Michael and Jeanne Harper were visiting St. Hugh's. About three weeks earlier I had been praying that the Lord would show us how to use this weekend to His glory. He gave me a vision of the school grounds next to the church, with hundreds of people milling about. It seemed that He wanted us to have a large conference there. At three weeks notice? If it was what the Lord wanted then it would be possible. On the Saturday nearly four hundred people from all over the diocese came to hear Michael and Jeanne talk about baptism in the Holy Spirit. To my delight, Caroline came to one of the sessions. The day ended with a time of worship in the church, when the Lord moved in a beautiful way and several people were filled with the Spirit.

That night, our son Clive had violent stomach pains. I was in no doubt that it was appendicitis. Caroline and I prayed — together! The pain persisted.

"You'd better call the doctor," I said.

In the early hours of Sunday morning Caroline and I took Clive to the hospital — together! All the way there I praised the Lord! I could not make myself anxious; I was perfectly at peace about the whole situation. I knew Clive was going to have surgery, and I didn't have the slightest trace of fear or anxiety about it. I love Clive, like my own self.

The doctors were concerned at the extent of the pain and decided to operate immediately. It seemed that once the decision was made, the pain eased considerably for little Clive. Being the hospital chaplain, I was allowed to go with him to the operating theatre. "Don't worry," the sister kept saying to me; but she was more anxious than I was.

I took Caroline home while the operation was taking place. There was no point in hanging around the hospital when the Lord was in charge of the situation! No sooner had I settled her with a cup of tea, than the telephone rang. It was the accident department of the hospital — I was wanted in my official capacity as chaplain.

While there, I went to the recovery ward to see Clive sleeping peacefully. His appendix had been removed, and all was well.

Nothing very astonishing about that! However, Clive's recovery was rather unusual. He was out of hospital on the following Wednesday and running about the garden as if nothing had happened on the Thursday. He would even have ridden his bicycle around the block, if we had allowed him!

Most important of all, something happened to Caroline in all this. Neither of us can remember exactly what happened or when it happened, but during the following week, she became quietly radiant — not just the lovely Caroline I had known. She was even lovelier as she had now become radiant with the Holy Spirit.

Suddenly we were together, we were one! — in the Spirit! My prayers had been answered and the Lord had fulfilled His promise. Alleluia!

Our marriage had been a pretty good one; we had never had a serious argument and we loved and trusted one another implicitly.

Now we had a new marriage and could enjoy a great new relationship. It seemed that the Lord had used the recent situation to take our natural marriage to the cross and crucify it. In return He had given us a resurrection-marriage. We loved one another more deeply than ever before. We prayed together and read the Scriptures together. And we shared our lives more fully.

Marriage "in the Spirit" is wonderful!

The Lord moves in strange ways sometimes! Some months later a homeless family of seven arrived in Luton. Although the vicarage was already full, it was suggested that they stayed with us until permanent accommodation could be found for them. "We'll manage somehow," Caroline said, "the Lord will make sure of that."

13 Gomer

JESUS WANTED US to be a community of love and praise. That would involve facing up to what it meant to be a disciple; being prepared to lay down everything for Christ. It was no use being content to live as happy Christians. We would discover even greater joy by being obedient to the leading of the Holy Spirit, allowing Him to take us into the realm of deeper commitment.

The weaknesses in our commitment and love for one another were being exposed in our failures.

Some of us had been made to realise that if our lives belonged to the Lord, then so did everything we had. Not everybody was eager to face up to this. The Spirit was having to do a great deal in the individual lives of the members of our church family, to prepare us for the baking process. Before we could become the Lord's new loaf, the flour would have to be sifted and the dough kneaded. When applied to human lives this process could be painful and demanding, as we all had to learn through Gomer's experience.

Gomer and I had become close friends. You may remember that he was the first to be baptised in the Spirit at St. Hugh's, and that he had real vision of the way the Lord wanted to work amongst us as a church family.

Soon after his re-election as churchwarden, Gomer began to get twitches of pain in his back and leg. He asked for prayer on one or two occasions and the pain went, but only

115

for a short time. It would return with greater intensity.

His doctor told him he had sciatica and that he was to rest. After some weeks he was admitted to hospital for observation. The first indication that anything serious was wrong came soon afterwards. Suddenly a brain tumour developed. Gomer lay in his hospital bed in a pitiful state. He was delirious and his body heaved about in an ugly way. The doctors expected him to be dead within forty-eight hours.

That same day a call went round the parish, summoning everybody to come together to pray that evening. The church was almost full, although it was the beginning of the annual holiday for the local factories. Every person who could possibly be present was there.

As I stood up to lead the prayer that night, I was conscious of the Lord's hand upon me. It never occurred to me to pray for anything other than Gomer's complete recovery; but we were made to face a great truth first.

The Lord showed us that as Gomer was a son of God, his life belonged to his heavenly Father. We had no rights and claims upon him. Our Father had the right to do as He pleased with His son.

We told the Lord that if He decided to raise Gomer to glory now, we would praise Him — and mean it! We told Him also of our love for our brother, and prayed that He might be healed and set back amongst us.

The following day Gomer was lying peacefully in his hospital bed. Apparently all the effects of the brain tumour had disappeared, although he was still not completely healed. The rest of his physical condition seemed to be unchanged.

Something was stirring deep down inside me. The Lord was going to teach something very important through Gomer, and I had a good idea what that lesson would be.

For the next five weeks he lay in hospital, the object of continual prayer by members of the family. Several people, away on holiday, would telephone Luton every day to keep in touch with the news about him. Through this situation the Lord was creating a deeper bond of love between us all.

Daily prayer meetings began in the mornings. We knew that it could be any one of us in that hospital bed, depending upon our brothers and sisters to support us in prayer.

Gomer himself believed in God's healing power. He had been healed of minor complaints during the previous three years; his wife, Audrey, had been healed of a spastic colon. He had laid hands on people himself and had seen them healed. He loved the Lord and prayed that He would cleanse him of every little thing that was alien to His purpose. Gomer was certainly going through the purifying fire now.

It was discovered that the brain tumour was only a secondary to the main cancer in Gomer's body. The Lord heeded our prayers; he was being spared all the pain normally associated with this dreadful disease, and he was filled with a patience and peace that could come only from the Holy Spirit.

We called the church family to a day of prayer with fasting. It was another sign of love, that the whole family responded to this, even though fasting was a new experience for many. We did not pray only for Gomer; we knew that, as a body, we needed to learn all the lessons the Lord was wanting to teach us through this situation.

Through Gomer's illness we were moving further towards what the Lord wanted us to be; a body of people bound together in love. Many of those who had argued against this life of commitment to one another now found themselves doing it quite naturally. But at what a cost!

Gomer continued to grow weaker. He was dying. I knew it. He knew it.

"Gomer," I said to him, "when you die, I shall be the most jealous man in Lewsey." I had experienced a taste of heaven, and I knew what I was talking about.

Gomer was already at one with the Lord — so there was nothing to fear in dying! To the last, he remained a great witness to the hospital staff. He could be a very impatient man, but throughout his illness he was filled with the patience that is a precious fruit of the Holy Spirit.

Only a few days before his death, he had the Roman

Catholic hospital chaplain on his knees at his bedside, while he prayed for him to be baptised in the Holy Spirit.

Apart from Audrey and the members of their family, no one was closer to Gomer during his illness than Peter. You may remember that they were hardly on speaking terms three years before. The Lord healed that relationship, and it was Peter who was such a strength to Audrey in the weeks after Gomer's death.

Audrey was also a witness. She showed little anxiety; instead she radiated peace. She spent much of her time quietly ministering to the people who came to visit her husband.

Gomer died peacefully on a Monday morning, early in September. During the previous week, the Lord had told me to call a meeting of the whole body of Christ at St. Hugh's on the following Thursday evening, but He didn't tell me why. At the Sunday services I asked everybody to come together on that evening. It so happened Gomer's funeral was arranged for the Friday morning; so on Thursday evening we had a thanksgiving Eucharist for our dear brother.

The church was crowded that night. I am not a very emotional person, but I wept all through that service. When I went up into the pulpit to give the address, I could hardly speak, and later I had to be careful that my tears did not fall into the chalice.

They were not tears of sorrow. They were tears of love. They were tears of gratitude for such a dear brother, and they were tears of joy, for I knew he was already with the Father.

The sense of praise and glory at that service cannot be put into words. There was joy in our hearts and voices as we sang:

> I am the Resurrection, I am the Life;
> He who believes in me,
> Even though he die,
> He shall live for ever,
> And I will raise him up at the last day.

The funeral service on the following morning was a continuation of the thanksgiving service, but without the tears. The sense of praise and glory apparently had a deep effect upon many of the non-Christian mourners. They were the only ones mourning; for we were caught up in the wonder of God's love.

"It was more like a wedding than a funeral," was one comment.

"A coronation service," said another.

Gomer's death made us realise how much it mattered to God that we fulfil His purpose for us. During his illness we had been made to share our lives more closely with one another. We were being moulded together in love.

We also had to ask ourselves some searching questions. Where was the power of Jesus in His Body at St. Hugh's? We were used to people being healed, not dying. Could we have done anything more to prevent his death? We had prayed, we had fasted and listened to the Lord. It seemed that even in Gomer's death we were being taught. The Lord had chosen to raise His son to glory and He had given us all a sense of that glory as we gave thanks for our brother. We had acknowledged that God had the right to do whatever He pleased with His son.

If we could say; "Lord fulfil your perfect will for Gomer," should we not also be praying, "Lord, do whatever you like with each one of us, so that you may use all of us for your purpose"? Or, were we all to wait until our deathbeds before we would be prepared to recognise God's sovereign authority in our own lives?

This word "authority" came to the forefront of our life at St. Hugh's, together with the words "rebellion" and "obedience".

Were we prepared to recognise the Lord's authority in our lives? If so, we needed to repent of all the rebellion against Him that still existed within us. We had to go through a period of deep introspection.

The Lord showed us that, individually, selfish desires still dominated parts of our lives. Many of us were still "conformed to this world", and all of us needed to be further transformed by the renewal of our minds (see Romans 12:2).

For a few weeks, it was difficult to praise the Lord together; even our worship seemed "heavy". Whenever we wanted to relax and rejoice in the Lord, He prevented us, and made us look at ourselves. No wonder! We were disobedient children and our Father was confronting us with our disobedience.

Many still did not want the Lord to have absolute authority. Areas of their lives were closed to Him. Some were still saying, "This is my way of life; please come and share it Lord." Instead we each needed to say, "I am yours Lord, I belong to you. I will live in the way you please, and do whatever you want."

Lovingly and gently, God was laying claim to the areas of disobedience; but the Spirit was being met with firm resistance in some quarters.

When the Lord touches someone on a raw spot, there is a natural tendency to project what He is saying on to other people, which can make us critical of them.

It is easy to acknowledge God's words when He is saying pleasant things; not so easy when He is shining His light into the dark recesses of our lives, revealing areas of disobedience to His Word.

The Lord showed us that if we were not prepared to accept the authority of the Word of God, and the leading of the Spirit within the Body of Christ, then we were rebelling against Him. He had placed His authority within the Body of Christ. As members of His Body we could not regard ourselves as free agents to do as we pleased. If we were committed to the Lord we were committed to a new way of life, centred upon Him.

It is one thing to be grateful that He has given us new life, it is another thing to hear Him saying that this leads to a new way of living. Some did not want to hear this, yet at every turn this was clearly what God was saying. A good deal of criticism was directed towards me.

While I was leading everyone into the life of the Spirit, into wonderful depths of love and joy, all were happy with the Lord and with me. As soon as I began to talk about loving one another in the same way that Jesus loves us, and about laying down our lives for our friends, there were those who said: "That's not the Lord; that's Colin's opinion."

It was not until after Gomer's death that we began to see the seriousness of such thinking. This was not discontent with me; it was discontent with God Himself and the way that He was leading us. This was rebellion against the purpose of Almighty God. I began to appreciate this, so did some others, but how could the situation be remedied? I could hardly stand up in the pulpit and say: "Some of you are feeling rebellious towards me and that means you are rebelling against the Lord." Some would miss the point completely and accuse me of thinking that only I was being led by the Spirit!

One Sunday morning I felt that I should get up earlier than usual to spend more time in prayer. During that time I was particularly conscious of the Lord's hand being upon me, although I had no idea what I was to speak about at Parish Communion.

When I stood up to preach I still did not know what I was going to say. After a short time of prayer, everybody sat down. There was silence. "What now, Lord?" I thought. For some strange reason I felt near to tears and would willingly have returned to my seat without speaking.

The Lord took over. I found myself talking very quietly. I cannot remember all that I said; the words were not coming from me, and everybody present was aware of that. There was not a movement anywhere. Although I can remember little of what was said that morning, after the service some quietly came to ask my forgiveness.

The Lord had made them realise that they had been criticising God because, in their hearts, they had not agreed with the way His Spirit was leading us. As He could not be openly criticised I was receiving the blame from those who felt that their comfortable lives were being threatened.

Such acts of reconciliation lead to deeper bonds of love. God had also been speaking to me that morning. At the end of the sermon I said: "Only one thing matters to me personally, that we, as the Body of Christ, fulfil the purpose that God has for us. It doesn't matter what personal sacrifice that involves."

For the remainder of the service, I was deep in prayer, speaking quietly in tongues, interceding for all my brothers and sisters at St. Hugh's. I was beseeching the Lord that He would make us obedient to Him in everything; that He would be glorified in His Body in Lewsey. It was this obedience that was crucial. God's purpose could never be fulfilled in our lives until we were willing to be obedient to Him. I told the Lord that I would be prepared to give myself, in any way necessary, to bring this about in the lives of my brothers and sisters. I would even be ready to be "accursed and cut off from Christ, for the sake of my brethren" (Romans 9:3).

There are verses of Scripture which most of us avoid because they seem beyond us. I had often thought about that verse from Romans, but could not believe that I would ever be able to apply it to myself. Having discovered the salvation of Jesus, having experienced something of the glory of heaven, it was unthinkable to sacrifice those joys for anyone. Periods of spiritual dryness, when God seemed very distant, were bad enough. To think in terms of eternal separation from God was unbearable.

Yet, just before receiving the bread and wine, I prayed those words — and meant them.

At our evening service Trevor, who had replaced David on the parish staff, was preaching. He began to speak about Moses leading the children of Israel out of the bondage of Egypt towards the Promised Land. Everybody followed him eagerly, until things became difficult in the wilderness, where the Hebrews were faced with their disobedience. I hardly knew where to put myself when Trevor continued:

"We have a wilderness situation here. Colin is like Moses. He led the members of this church family out of bondage into a new life in the Spirit. But when the Lord began to reveal His real purpose for us, some didn't like it. As the Israelites blamed Moses, so there are those among us who have blamed Colin, instead of facing up to the rebellion in their hearts and the disobedience in their lives."

These words convinced many who had not been at the morning service and led to a time of repentance and submission to the Lord.

I was moved to share with everyone what had happened to me that morning. I have never been hugged so often as I was at the end of the service, when people left the church. A deeper bond of love was created between us all as more of us faced up to God's authority in our lives.

This was the most important single day in the history of our church. Since then, our hearts have once again been filled with joy as we delight in praising the Lord together. And more of the Lord's power is being released among us in different ways.

14 To Be Continued

JESUS SAID: "You are my friends if you do what I command you." He said this immediately after telling the disciples: "This is my commandment, that you love one another as I have loved you. Greater love has no man than this, that a man lay down his life for his friends" (John 15:14, 12, 13).

We were beginning to understand what that meant; if we needed a vision of where the Lord was leading, we would have to look no further than the Acts of the Apostles. Wherever the renewal of the Church is taking place today, the opening verses of chapter two are quoted and requoted. They tell of the way in which the Holy Spirit came upon those early Christians, gathered together on the day of Pentecost.

However, few are so keen to quote the closing verses of that same chapter, which give a brief account of the kind of life that the Holy Spirit produced among the first Christian community in Jerusalem.

> And all who believed were together, and had all things in common; and they sold their possessions and goods, and distributed them to all, as any had need. And day by day attending the temple together, and breaking bread in their houses, they partook of food with glad and generous hearts, praising God and having favour with all the people. And the Lord added to their number day by day those who were being saved (Acts 2: 44–47).

At St. Hugh's we came naturally into the experience of Pentecost, as we sought reality and power in our Christian lives. And now the Lord is leading us naturally into the sharing together of a common life.

Several families now share their lives together in as complete a way as possible. This involves, not only having fellowship together "in the Spirit", but sharing the practical and material aspects of living. For example, the entire income of these families is given to the Lord. All property and possessions are held "in common".

Those who have the responsibility of administering the finances of this "common life", see that these families' needs are met. However, as much money as possible is released for the Lord's work and is used, in particular, to support several lay people working full-time in the parish, and taking part in the ministry that our church has in sharing the life of the Spirit with Christians of other churches.

We are all one and each has his function within the common life of the Body of Christ. That may mean a person leaving secular employment, if God gives him or her a full-time ministry to fulfil. It may mean remaining in secular employment and sharing all one's resources to support such ministries.

One of our young housewives had bought a small van and went round the local housing estates selling vegetables. When the Lord first began to talk to us about sharing our lives together, she believed that God wanted to use the vegetable van.

Peter, the first layman to leave his employment and make all his time available to the Lord, organised a group of ladies to drive the van, sell the vegetables and meet any needs that arose in the process of doing this. The idea was to establish contact with the elderly, handicapped and housebound people in our district. Peter and the ladies found that opportunities arose to help in practical ways many of those on whom they called. As business was not the real objective, they would often be delayed on their round because they stopped and listened to people's problems. Whenever the opportunity arose, they would talk about Jesus or offer to pray with people.

As time went on, they spent more time witnessing and praying — and less time selling vegetables. The van was sold as being superfluous, but we were left with a different problem: how to cope with all the contacts we had made! There is a limit to the amount of time housewives can spend in such work, if they have children and a home to care for.

This underlined for us the necessity to have more people available to work full-time in our area.

It is totally unrealistic to leave all the pastoral work in the church to its few ordained members. As the Lord is teaching us to share in the outreach of the church, so He is also raising up those within the Body who are sensitive to the leading of the Spirit and to the personal needs of people. They are beginning to help with counselling and the prayer ministry.

When the Lord spoke to us about authority, He made it quite clear that we needed to revise our traditional concepts of authority within the local Body of Christ. There are so many weighty decisions requiring spiritual rather than practical insight. As we recognised our need in this direction and prayed about it, so the Lord began to raise up lay people who could share in the spiritual responsibilities of our church family. Again, these have needed to be those who would make their lives available to the Lord, so that they can be "the willing servants of all".

Our way of life, and our church life, is continuing to change. It no longer makes sense for us to talk about "my life" or "our lives," for "we are all one person in Christ Jesus" (Gal. 3:28 NEB), sharing a common life within His Body. Certainly, it is difficult to remember what it was like to be part of St. Hugh's four years ago, when we all came to church on Sundays and attended the occasional mid-week meeting. Only a few members of our church have wanted that kind of church life.

We were given a vision of all the members of our family standing in circles within the church building. These were circles of commitment. Some would choose to stand in the outermost circle, on the fringe of things; others in the innermost circle, sharing a common life together; others would choose one of the intermediary circles. We were shown that it is of importance that everybody should feel free to stand in the circle of their own choice, and also be free to move from one circle to another. None of us was to be critical of any other person's decision as to where to stand.

Each one of us needs to face Jesus as He says to us: "This is my commandment, that you love one another as I have loved you. Greater love has no man than this, that a man lay down his life for his friends. You are my friends if you do what I command you" (John 15: 12–14).

Jesus said these words within the context of His teaching.

"You are to love one another that the world might believe," the Lord told us at St. Hugh's. And that is only a reflection of what He is telling us in His Word.

We were not a very old church, but we needed to be renewed in love. We could not choose the way to be renewed; only the Lord could do that. He wanted to baptise us in the Holy Spirit; we allowed him to do so. He wanted to share with us the gifts of the Holy Spirit; we gratefully accepted them and it is certain that the renewal of our church would not be taking place without the use of these gifts. He wanted to lead us into a new commitment to one another in love so that the world around us might believe; after some rebellion we are allowing Him to do that now.

He is wanting . . . What is He wanting next? Whatever the answer to that question, I pray that it will contain as much blessing and joy as we have experienced together in the last four years. Knowing something of the way our Father works, the blessings to come will be immeasurably greater!